D0289951

I Don't Want a Divorce

I Don't Want a Divorce

A 90 DAY GUIDE TO SAVING YOUR MARRIAGE

Dr. David Clarke

with WILLIAM G. CLARKE

Revell

a division of Baker Publishing Group
Grand Rapids, Michigan

© 2009 by David Clarke & William G. Clarke

Published by Revell
a division of Baker Publishing Group
P.O. Box 6287, Grand Rapids, MI 49516-6287
www.revellbooks.com

Printed in the United States of America

All rights reserved. No part of this publication may be reproduced, stored in a retrieval system, or transmitted in any form or by any means—for example, electronic, photocopy, recording—without the prior written permission of the publisher. The only exception is brief quotations in printed reviews.

Library of Congress Cataloging-in-Publication Data
Clarke, David, Dr.
    I don't want a divorce : a 90 day guide to saving your marriage / Dr. David Clarke, with William G. Clarke.
        p. cm.
    ISBN 978-0-8007-3401-5 (pbk.)
    1. Spouses—Religious life. 2. Marriage—Religious aspects—Christianity. 3. Communication in marriage. 4. Divorce—Prevention. I. Clarke, William G. II. Title.
BV4596.M3C574 2009
248.8′44—dc22   2009021608

Unless otherwise indicated, Scripture is taken from the HOLY BIBLE, NEW INTER-NATIONAL VERSION®. NIV®. Copyright © 1973, 1978, 1984 by International Bible Society. Used by permission of Zondervan. All rights reserved.

Scripture marked NASB is taken from the New American Standard Bible®, Copyright © 1960, 1962, 1963, 1968, 1971, 1972, 1973, 1975, 1977, 1995 by The Lockman Foundation. Used by permission.

Published in association with Joyce Hart of the Hartline Literary Agency, LLC.

To protect the privacy of those whose stories are shared by the author, some details and names have been changed.

14   15   16   8   7   6

In keeping with biblical principles of creation stewardship, Baker Publishing Group advocates the responsible use of our natural resources. As a member of the Green Press Initiative, our company uses recycled paper when possible. The text paper of this book is comprised of 30% post-consumer waste.

To Bob and Pam Johns,
two great friends,
two great teachers,
and one great example of what staying in love
is all about.

Contents

Part 1 Yes, You Can Change Your Marriage

   1. The Good News about a Bad Marriage 11

Part 2 The "We're Unhappy but Willing to Work on It" Marriage

   2. "Take Your Marriage Out Back and Shoot It!" 25
     Week 1 *Rebuild from the Ground Up* 26

   3. "I'm Wrong, I'm Sorry, I'll Change" 38
     Week 2 *The Letter of Responsibility* 45
     Week 3 *Do the Top Two* 51

   4. Where the Rubber Meets the Road: One Couple's Journey through Weeks 2 and 3 53

   5. A Breath of Fresh, Positive Air 65
     Week 4 *The Power of Positivity* 69

   6. A Little Bit of Romance Goes a Long Way 78
     Week 5 *Bring Back the Romance* 81

   7. Conflict-Resolving Skills That Work 90
     Week 6 *Learn How to Fight* 92

   8. Heal from Your Past Pain 103
     Week 7 *The Past Pain Transfer Letters* 110
     Week 8 *The Follow-Up Talks* 116

Contents

9. The Pain Is Gone and We're Moving On: One Couple's Journey through Weeks 7 and 8   118

10. Forgive Each Other   129

    Week 9 *The Letters of Forgiveness*   134

    Week 10 *Read and Follow-Up Talks*   136

11. "I Forgive You": One Couple's Journey through Weeks 9 and 10   140

12. The Code Queen and the Clam   151

    Week 11 *Make Your Needs Clear*   157

13. To Be Soul Mates, You Have to Be "Need Mates"   162

    Week 12 *Meet Your Top Three Needs*   165

Part 3 The "My Spouse Won't Change" Marriage

14. "I Married a Stick and Now I'm Stuck"   179

15. Your Stick's Last Chance   190

16. Rock Your Stick's World   204

Part 4 The "My Spouse Has Sinned Big Time" Marriage

17. Make Your Spouse's Serious Sin the Only Issue   219

18. Get Angry and Stay Angry   230

19. How to Heal from a Spouse's Serious Sin   241

Part 5 With God and a Proven Plan, It's Time to Change Your Marriage

20. Killing Your Goliath   261

    Frequently Asked Questions   267
    Appendix: Beginning a Relationship with God   273

Part 1

Yes, You Can Change Your Marriage

1

The Good News
about a Bad Marriage

Your marriage is in trouble. That's why you picked up this book. You're not happy. Your spouse isn't happy. Your marriage is not on the right track. Needs are not being met. You never thought your marriage would get to this. But it has.

You don't want a divorce.

You want intimacy. You want passion. You want to feel in love again. And the sooner the better.

If you're in a marriage that needs to be saved, I have good news and more good news.

The Good News

The first piece of good news is that you are not alone. You and your spouse are part of a huge club with millions of members. Just about every marriage breaks down and ends up in trouble. It is the nature of the beast.

In 1 Corinthians 7:28, the apostle Paul has this to say about marriage:

Those who marry will face many troubles in this life.

Yeah. No kidding. I almost used these ten words as the title of this book. Paul is communicating a universal truth: Every married couple will be forced to deal with many difficulties.

You fall in love. Neither one of you has a clue about the problems that will begin to hit you just a few years into marriage—sometimes just a few months into marriage. This naïve ignorance is a blessing. If any of us had the slightest inkling of the potholed road ahead, no one would ever get married. The human race would die quickly.

With bright eyes and bright hopes, you get married. Your hormone-driven passion peters out eighteen months after the wedding day. Your male-female differences, annoying habits, and ever-increasing conflicts put a pounding on your love. Add a child or two and now you're really in for it.

You spend less and less time together. You don't talk on a deep level. You can't remember the last personal conversation you had. Romance and affection are way down. Sex is infrequent and not too exciting. You fight more and more and can't resolve disagreements. Or worse, you avoid conflicts by avoiding each other and touchy subjects.

Sound familiar? This progressive breakdown in a marriage happens to 99.99 percent of all couples who tie the knot. Including my wife, Sandy, and me. If you are in that .01 percent of couples who have weathered the storms without breaking down, congratulations. I mean it. You are the extraordinary exception.

If your marriage is good, and you want to make it better, this book isn't for you. Give it to a couple who needs it. If your marriage is currently bad and you want to make it better, a lot better, this book is for you.

The Three Troubled Marriages

So the question is not, "Is your marriage struggling?" We've established that it is. The two questions to be answered are: "How is your marriage struggling?" and "What can you do about it?"

As a clinical psychologist in private practice for more than twenty-three years, specializing in marital therapy, I have answers to both these questions.

The answer to the first question is this: Almost all troubled marriages fall into one of three categories.

The "We're Unhappy but Willing to Work on It" Marriage

Your marriage is not doing well, but neither of you has taken serious, damaging actions. And you both are willing to take steps to improve your relationship.

Marriages in this category, unhappy but experiencing no outrageous or deeply harmful behavior, tend to come in four types. See if you recognize yours.

"WE'RE OKAY."

Your marriage is okay. Fair. Mediocre. You're comfortable with each other. You feel stable and secure. What you don't feel is passion. Oh, you still love each other. But the thrill is gone.

Your marriage is based on commitment and routine, not intimacy. You're not sweethearts anymore. Your sex is still fairly frequent, but it is a five on a scale of one to ten. You work at your careers. You take care of the kids. You do household chores. You pay the bills. You visit your families. Exciting? No. Predictable and boring? Oh yeah.

Even though you're not terribly unhappy, you still have a bad marriage. It is far less than what it could be, and you know it. You are settling for a go-kart when you could have a Corvette. Being okay with an okay marriage is not okay. If you don't change your marriage pretty quickly, it will get worse. A lot worse. And it won't take a long time.

"We're Not Okay."

Your marriage is in trouble, and you are aware of it. No one has made a move toward divorce. In fact, no one has mentioned divorce. But you're both unhappy. Your feelings of love are greatly diminished. There are more negatives than positives in the relationship.

You are often irritated by your spouse's annoying habits and weaknesses. You are having more and more conflicts, usually over petty issues. You don't have deep, intimate, revealing conversations. You rarely go out on romantic dates. You're not playful with each other. Your kisses are stale, forced, and pathetically weak. Sex still happens sporadically, but it is more about meeting a biological need than about expressing love.

You're beginning to lead separate lives. You are avoiding each other. Your relationship doesn't give you energy. It sucks the energy and life right out of you. You're staying together because of commitment and because of the children.

You're not sure how much longer you can hold on. You've thought about divorce, even though you really don't want one. You find yourself wondering what it would be like to split up and be on your own. You begin to notice members of the opposite sex and find yourself attracted to them.

You don't realize it, but unless you are totally committed to following God's direction, you are an affair waiting to happen. Your marriage isn't dead yet, but it is in intensive care on life support.

"We're Miserable."

Your marriage has suffered a complete breakdown. It's dead. It's over. There are no feelings of love left. I call this kind of relationship *Dead Marriage Walking*.

You want out of your marriage. Or your spouse wants out. Divorce has been mentioned, probably many times. One spouse has filed for divorce or is on the verge of filing.

One spouse may have uttered those five horrible words: "I don't love you anymore." You are leading largely separate lives. There is very little interaction. You don't see any hope for your marriage. It's only a matter of time before it is ended. An affair may be happening or be close to happening.

You realize you have to do something, and quickly, or you'll either become more miserable or get divorced.

"It's All about the Kids."

Since the birth of your first child, your marriage has never been the same. You went from soul mates to superparents overnight. The product of your love has become the central focus of your love.

You are Mom and Dad 24/7. Diapers. Bottles. Toys. Strollers. Pacifiers. Playing with the kids. Reading stories. Homework. School events. Trips to see family. Vacations. Little visitors who come to your bed in the night. Children's television shows and family-friendly videos and DVDs. Watching their activities and sports.

Your kids have become more important—a lot more important—than your marriage. Most of your time, energy, and attention go to the kids. Most of your joy comes from the kids. You are making the mistake of thinking parenting is the most important thing that you can do. But the truth is, *loving each other is the most important thing that you can do.*

Kids are important, but they are number two. Number one is your marriage. When your marriage takes a backseat to anyone or anything else except the Lord, it suffers great harm. Your marriage is dying, and you may not even realize it.

The "My Spouse Won't Change" Marriage

Your spouse seems content with your marriage, even though it's lousy and has very little deep satisfaction or intimacy in it. He wants to stay with you and has no desire to divorce you, but he will do nothing to improve the relationship. Occasionally, he'll make a lame, half-hearted attempt to do some things differently, but it never lasts long.

You know what you're missing and are willing to do whatever it takes to enrich your marriage. You ask him to go to a marriage seminar. He says no. You ask him to read a marriage book like this one. He says no. You ask him to see your pastor or a Christian therapist. He says no. Even if he "tries" one of these options, he makes zero changes.

You are sick and tired of hearing his "no" to your every attempt to make some progress in your relationship. You wonder, "How can I motivate my slug of a husband to want to work on our marriage?"

The "My Spouse Has Sinned Big Time" Marriage

Your spouse has committed a serious, major sin, and you are reeling from the impact.

You have just discovered the sin or have finally had enough of a chronic, long-standing pattern of sinful behavior.

Sin is an ugly, nasty word. But it is the only word I can use to describe a behavior that shatters the trust of a spouse and breaks that person's heart into a million pieces. It is the only word God used to describe a behavior that inflicts such terrible damage on a spouse, a marriage, and a family. When I use the word *sin*, I'm talking about major, huge, massive offenses that tear apart the very core of a marriage.

He has committed adultery. (I'll use the male pronoun in these categories for convenience, although the woman could be the serious sinner.) He has been viewing pornography. He has been abusing alcohol and/or drugs. He has a nasty temper and has been verbally abusive to you. He has been physically abusing you. He is a workaholic. He has a gambling addiction. He has made terrible and costly, reckless and irresponsible financial mistakes. He has controlled every area of your life. He refuses to work hard at a career.

The only thing that gives you hope is that your spouse wants to stop sinning, stay with you, and work on the marriage.

You wonder, though, "How can we heal from the trauma of the sin and build a new marriage?"

More Good News

Is your marriage in one of these three categories? Are you asking yourself that second question, "What can I do about it?" This brings me to the second piece of good news about your struggling marriage:

I have a 90-Day Guide to Saving Your Marriage.

I didn't come up with this phrase because it makes a catchy title. I do have a plan. I've used it with hundreds of married couples in my clinical practice over the past twenty years. I know it works. *It can save your marriage by changing your marriage.*

Let me be clear. *Saving your marriage* is very important. That's the purpose of this book. But I don't want, and I'm sure you don't want, to simply avoid divorce and be stuck in the same old miserable marriage. I'm going to help you avoid divorce by changing your marriage into a marriage that really works.

So for the rest of this book, I'll be using these words: *Change Your Marriage.*

A Do-It-Yourself Program

This 90-day program is designed to be used by you and your spouse on your own. It is a step-by-step program that the two of you can follow without any outside help (except God and your accountability partners). If, however, after the 90 days, during which you diligently and fully followed the steps, you don't experience at least some significant improvement in the major issues hurting your marriage, please see your pastor or a licensed Christian therapist for additional guidance.

If you are a pastor or are involved in a ministry to hurting couples, I think you'll find this program very helpful in your counseling work. When your spouse and you try this, you will better understand how it can help others.

Change in Twelve Weeks

Ninety days is twelve weeks. I see couples in therapy once a week, so my plan unfolds over the course of twelve weeks. Here's a brief overview of my Change Your Marriage in Twelve Weeks Plan:

Week 1: Rebuild from the Ground Up

A solid foundation is critically important to building a brand-new marriage. Your building blocks are (1) God, (2) Accountability Partners, and (3) regular Couple Talk Times.

Weeks 2 and 3: "I'm Wrong, I'm Sorry, I'll Change"

Focusing on your spouse's faults won't get you anywhere. Identifying and working on *your* faults will produce the beginning of change.

Weeks 4 and 5: Pump In the Positives

Your marriage has enough negatives. You are in desperate need of positives to provide momentum, hope, and healing. Caring behaviors, compliments, communication skills, small romantic behaviors, and praying together will create positive, healthy connections. Only by *following the steps* and *experiencing them* will you see them work.

Week 6: Learn How to Fight

All couples have conflict. Very few know how to successfully resolve it. With some tried-and-true conflict-resolution skills, you and your spouse will be able to work through your past and current conflicts and gain the tools for your future conflicts.

Weeks 7 and 8: Heal from Your Past Pain

Both of you have unresolved pain from your pasts. Your pain is connected to people: parents, siblings, other family members, friends, teachers, coaches or other authority figures, neighbors, old boyfriends or girlfriends, and ex-spouses. This pain transfers to your spouse and damages your marriage. Together, you can heal from your pain and eliminate the transfer.

Weeks 9 and 10: Forgive Each Other

You've done and said things to hurt each other over the years. These hurts have continued to fester and do incredible damage to your relationship. It's time to clean out your resentments, truly forgive, and move ahead with a clean slate.

Weeks 11 and 12: Meet Your Deepest Needs

To have a great marriage, your real needs must be met on a regular basis. I'll show you how to communicate your emotional, physical, and spiritual needs and have them met.

How to Use the Book

Depending on which category of troubled marriage you're in, here's how you navigate through this Change Your Marriage program:

If you're in the "We're Unhappy but Willing to Work on It" marriage, you read Chapters 2 through 13. These chapters contain my twelve-week Change Your Marriage program. You can skip Chapters 14 through 19 and then read Chapter 20.

If you're in this first category, "We're Unhappy but Willing to Work on It," and your spouse won't read the book, no problem. You read it first, and then guide your reading-challenged spouse through the steps of my program. If your spouse won't read the book *and* refuses to follow the Change Your Marriage steps, you automatically shift into the "My Spouse Won't Change" marriage, and you follow that route through the book.

If you're in the "My Spouse Won't Change" marriage, by definition you will read and do this twelve-week program on your own. Read Chapter 2 and complete the steps for Week 1. Then read Chapters 3 through 13 to understand the six additional steps, and read Chapters 14 through 16 for specific instructions on how to motivate your stubborn spouse to change. You can skip Chapters 17 through 19 and finish by reading Chapter 20.

Living with a spouse who refuses to change is an ongoing nightmare. I'm going to help you end the nightmare using biblical, practical, tough-love action steps. After completing each of the program's seven steps, you'll ask your spouse to also complete that step. If your spouse will not do any of the steps, it's time to bring out the heavy, biblical artillery.

Your difficult and stupid (the Bible refers to this person as a fool) spouse will be backed into a corner and forced to make a decision. Your foolish spouse will change or not change, but you will be content knowing that you have done all God wanted you to do and that he empowered you to do in the marriage.

If you're in the "My Spouse Has Sinned Big Time" marriage, start with Chapter 2 and complete Week 1's steps. Then jump ahead and read and apply Chapters 17 through 19 to begin to concentrate on the process of healing from the sin's traumatic impact. After that you'll be prepared to go back and read Chapters 3 through 13 and do the rest of my Change Your Marriage steps. You'll finish by reading Chapter 20, the final chapter, and reading my closing words of motivation and—hopefully—inspiration.

You may ask, "What if my sinning spouse refuses to follow your steps of healing?" My answer, which involves some heavy-duty tough love, is found in Chapter 19.

It's Time for a Change

You're sick of your marriage. You ought to be. It's not working. It's broken down. It's painful rather than joyful. It's time to leave your old marriage behind. Stop your car, dump your marriage on the side of the road, and move on. You're not going back to it.

What you can do is build a brand-new marriage with your current spouse.

I consider it a sacred privilege to work with married couples whose relationships are in trouble, who are being robbed of joy in this most important of human relationships. I have the greatest job in the world. I get to help couples to refuse to get a divorce and to follow the steps of healing and recovery and restored happiness. I get to see God at work and to watch couples fall in love again and create a healthy, God-inspired, God-maintained intimacy.

I thank God for the hundreds of success stories I've been involved with over the years of my practice and in my seminar ministry. (I've provided tools and impetus; the couples did the work.)

The principles in this book helped Sandy and me get through some difficult periods in our relationship. We've been married since 1982, and our love continues to get stronger and deeper.

I thank God in advance for what he's going to do for your marriage.

Paul, quoting Genesis 2:24, records this wonderful definition of marriage:

> For this reason a man will leave his father and mother and be united to his wife, and the two will become one flesh.
>
> Ephesians 5:31

These two words, *one flesh*, describe a deeply intimate and passionate marriage relationship expressed physically, emotionally, and spiritually.

This is the kind of marriage God wants you and your spouse to have. It's the kind of marriage God wants every couple to have.

No matter where your marriage is now, you can change it into becoming this kind of marriage.

In twelve weeks.

Part 2

The "We're Unhappy but Willing to Work on It" Marriage

2

"Take Your Marriage Out Back and Shoot It!"

I'm sitting in my therapy office with a married couple. It's near the end of my first session with them. They've just described all the painful struggles they're having in their relationship. They pause and look at me for words of hope, motivation, and wisdom. They're paying a considerable fee for the words about to come out of my mouth.

I lean forward and tell them what I tell every married couple at the end of a first session: "Well, your marriage is over. Done. Dead. Finished. Kaput. Finito. We can't save it. Frankly, it's not worth saving. Take it out back and shoot it."

The couple is shocked. Stunned. One of them blurts out in an angry, exasperated voice: "Are you kidding? What do you mean, it's over? We came here for help!"

Before they can leave in a huff and not pay me, I say: "Wait a minute. I'm not done yet. Your old marriage is over. That's the one I want you to shoot and bury. What we've got to do is build a brand-new marriage. One that works. One that God has always wanted you to enjoy. With God's help, and my twelve-week program, we can do it."

Rebuild from the Ground Up

Your marriage is like a house that has been torn down. Without meaning to, you have torn it down yourselves, since you *are* the marriage. The rebuilding process must begin with a solid foundation. Your new foundation contains three pillars supporting it.

In the next week, which I call Week 1, you'll begin working on these three pillars. You'll continue to work on them for the entire twelve-week process and for the rest of your married lives. That's right. They are that important.

God

You need to begin now—right now—improving and strengthening your relationship with God. The words that John the Baptist said of Jesus must become your words: "He must become greater; I must become less" (John 3:30). Chances are very good that your spiritual life has been weakened by your marriage problems. Marital conflict weakens every area of your life. So if you're not spiritually strong right now, you're normal.

But you need to get back in the spiritual saddle with God. Your success in this program depends, to a large degree, on your spirituality (i.e., how close each of you is to the Lord, and how close you are to him as a couple; this is accomplished by spiritual disciplines that I will describe later in the book).

> Unless the LORD builds the house,
> its builders labor in vain.
>
> Psalm 127:1

> I am the vine; you are the branches. If a man remains in me and I in him, he will bear much fruit; apart from me you can do nothing.
>
> John 15:5

Pretty clear, isn't it? Any endeavor attempted on your own will fail. Any endeavor attempted with God, that honors him, will succeed.

Now, before you panic, let me assure you that you don't need to be some spiritual giant any time soon. God knows that you're hurting and that growing spiritually may be hard for you. The words of Jesus describe the awesome power of a tiny amount of faith:

> I tell you the truth, if you have faith as small as a mustard seed, you can say to this mountain, "Move from here to there" and it will move. Nothing will be impossible for you.
>
> Matthew 17:20

A mustard seed is incredibly small! All God asks is that you try to move toward him. Make the effort. Take some action steps. He will do the rest.

What God Will Do for You

- With his help, you can create deep, lasting change in yourself and in your marriage.
- With his help, you can think positively about your spouse.
- With his help, you will have the strength to get through my tough twelve-week program.
- With his help, you will fall in love again.
- With his help, you and your spouse will win the spiritual battle for your marriage.

It's Three against Satan

Don't think for a second that Satan is not actively and aggressively attacking your marriage. He hates God. He hates you. If you have kids, he hates them. He hates your marriage and will do anything to destroy it. His name means adversary. You certainly do your part to damage the relationship, but Satan is also blazing away with everything he has in his arsenal.

You are in a vicious, intense spiritual battle for your marriage. Satan wants you to get divorced. Or, failing that, he'll settle for you having a miserable marriage. God wants you to stay married and enjoy a terrific, as-long-as-you-live love story.

If you expect to win this battle, you each must work to grow closer to God. If it's only you and your spouse against Satan, you'll lose. If it's you and your spouse and God against Satan, you'll win. And you'll win big. "The one who is in you [the Holy Spirit] is greater than the one who is in the world [Satan]" (1 John 4:4).

A Daily Time with God

Spend time with God every day. Just you and God in a quiet place. This could be early in the morning, before you go to bed, or on your lunch break. Talk with him. Thank him for all he has done for you. Praise and adore him for who he is. Tell him the honest truth about your personal and marital pain. Make specific requests. Ask him for help in applying this book's steps, and ask him to help your spouse apply the steps.

Read the Bible and meditate on it. Be quiet and listen to what God is saying to you through his Word and the Holy Spirit. God's Word has the power to change you and keep you changed.

Regular Church Attendance

God wants you and your spouse in church on a regular basis. He has chosen the local church as his vehicle to change the world. God commands believers not to get out of the habit of attending church (Heb. 10:25), but to be committed and active members of a local church (Acts 2:42; Eph. 4:14–16).

You need a local church that will support you emotionally and spiritually as you work to change your marriage. You need a church where you can find accountability partners. You need a church where the Bible is taught from the pulpit. You need a church where you can be in a Sunday Bible class, a women's or men's Bible study and fellowship group, a support group, or a life group where you will receive the encouragement and emotional connections that smaller groups like these provide. You need a church where you and your family can worship God and serve him with your gifts.

Though not essential, it is preferable to be in a church with a strong men's ministry, a strong women's ministry, and a strong marriage ministry. A church with these programs can meet your relational needs, expose you to good Christian role models, and provide biblical teaching on how to build a great marriage.

Come to Christ

I would love for you to know God as we embark on this journey of change together. If you don't know God yet—

except perhaps as a "force," a distant mystery figure, a punitive judge, or a doddering old grandfather—now would be a great time to begin a relationship with him.

It's only through Jesus Christ that you can connect with God.

> Salvation is found in no one else, for there is no other name under heaven given to men by which we must be saved.
>
> Acts 4:12

(If you want to know more about beginning a personal relationship with God through Jesus, please see the appendix in the back of this book. I place this in an appendix, though it is the very first priority in life. Please go to the appendix now if you so desire.)

I hope you know God through Jesus as you begin this journey of marital change.

But if you don't, I pray you will meet him along the way.

One Accountability Partner for Each of You

The second pillar in your new relationship foundation is accountability. You and your spouse each need to find a person who will serve as an accountability partner. My Change Your Marriage program is difficult. It will make a big difference to have a same-sex confidant(e) to walk beside you every step of the way.

Here's your accountability partner's job description:

- loves Jesus
- loves you
- is not a family member
- can keep secrets
- will confront you without hesitation or reservation
- will comfort

- will encourage
- will listen
- will make time on a regular basis to talk and pray with you

This person may be your age or older or younger. This person may already be a friend or may be someone you have not met. Preferably, he or she will be married—and, from everything you know and observe, *happily* married. Your partner's marriage may not be perfect, of course, but it should be strong, stable, healthy, and growing better. Your relationship with this person may be one-way, with your friend serving as a mentor to you, or it may be a mutual relationship with the two of you holding each other accountable for the Change Your Marriage Steps.

I recommend a once-a-week, face-to-face meeting with your accountability partner. Never use mail or email to discuss personal things that are going on in your marriage. The meeting should be in a quiet and private setting and should last at least an hour. You will discuss the specific Change Your Marriage Steps you are working on and the obstacles you are encountering in the change process. End each meeting with prayer.

Use phone contact as needed to keep your communication current. Sometimes you will need to vent or ask for a shot of encouragement between meetings. That's what phones and accountability partners are for. Make these calls, and don't feel guilty about doing so. However, save intensely personal things for your in-person meetings.

Start thinking right now about who can be your accountability partner. Make a list of candidates. Pray that God will direct you to the right person. If you can't think of anyone, go to your pastor and ask him to help you find someone. For a variety of reasons, sometimes it can be very difficult to find this person. But God will help you if you don't give up. When you have identified one or more possibilities, summon your courage and go to these individuals and ask them to serve in this accountability role. The right person will be willing and will see it as a kindness to a brother or sister and as a way to serve the Lord.

If you don't have an accountability partner now, go ahead and begin the program anyway. An accountability partner is not essential for successful marital change, but this kind of "I've got your back" friend is very, very helpful. For some, however, it could make the difference between success and failure. It is very easy for us to lie to ourselves and to rationalize our behavior. Without a partner to hold us to the truth and confront us, we may find it easy to justify our actions and thwart the Change Your Marriage program. Keep praying and looking for your accountability partner as you move through the twelve-week process. At some point, it's very likely God will lead you to the right person.

Four Couple Talk Times per Week

The third pillar is establishing and maintaining four twenty-to-thirty-minute Couple Talk Times per week. This is an essential part of my program. Without it, your marriage will not change. With it, you will have a great opportunity to experience real change in your relationship.

Time together is the foundation of every intimate relationship. Time does not guarantee intimacy, but it is absolutely necessary for intimacy to be created. Despite conflictual or bad feelings between you now or in the past, do this. Ask the Lord, and trust him that you can begin talking again and reconnect.

When you make time to be together, you can produce some positive flow in your relationship and begin the process of reconnecting as a couple. As your marriage breaks down, the amount of time you spend together becomes less and less. You become masters at avoiding each other. Where you found that talking together was fun and drew you closer, now you don't find talking a pleasure. Even if it is awkward and forced at first, regular time together gets you on track to rebuilding your marriage.

When you make time to be together, you can begin to spiritually bond as a couple. God is willing and able and eager to help you in your marital recovery. But to get his help, you must include him in your relationship. Growing spiritually as individuals is important. Growing spiritually as a couple is equally important.

When you make time to be together, you can work on and improve every area of your marriage. In your Couple Talk Times, you'll be practicing the skills needed to rebuild your relationship. A significant part of the Change Your Marriage program takes place during these talk times.

Doing these talk times will be very, very difficult. Don't wait until you feel like doing them. That will never happen. Force yourself to do it. Sit down and talk because it is the right thing to do. Because you have to. Because I'm the doctor, and I'm telling you it is a necessity. Because God wants you to do it. God will honor your obedience. He *is* love (1 John 4:8) and will pour his love out on you both.

What Couple Talk Time Looks Like

Sit down over the weekend and schedule your couple times for the upcoming week. Nail down specific days and times. Take into consideration any activities that might prevent these times, and put them on your calendars and day planners and in your PDAs. Don't wing it and hope to pull off these meetings without planning. Without planning, they'll never happen. Schedule them.

Make it your goal to meet every day. Life will probably prevent you from meeting seven days a week, but by aiming high, you will be able to squeeze in the highest possible number of couple times. I tell my clients, "Shoot for seven and get four." A minimum of four couple times a week will be enough to generate connection and closeness.

Pick the times that are best for both of you (not always an easy task). It doesn't matter when you meet as long as you sit together for twenty to thirty minutes during the day. It could be in the morning, at lunchtime, or in the evening. If you choose the evening, be sure to meet as early as possible. You want to be fresh and alert. Don't meet just before bed, because a couple of exhausted, brain-dead spouses can't produce any intimacy.

Where you meet is also important. It must be private and quiet. Send your children to their rooms with strict instructions not to come out until you give them the high sign. Choose a comfortable place like the living room or the den or the back porch. Soft, low lighting will help create the proper ambience.

I recommend that you not have your couple times in bed. It's too relaxing. Lying or reclining will make you drowsy. When one partner falls asleep, it kind of ruins the couple time. Besides, the husband may "accidentally" go into fondling mode, and it's hard to fondle and talk at the same time. The bed is for sleeping and sex, not for talking. If you can sit in comfortable chairs in your bedroom, that would work just fine.

Screen out all distractions during these couple times. No television. No computer. No kids. No pets. Don't answer the telephone or the door. You are escaping from the world and all its diversions during this sacred couple time.

The Husband Leads

In case you're wondering which spouse has the responsibility to lead in these Couple Talk Times, Ephesians 5:22–24 makes it crystal clear:

> Wives, submit to your husbands as to the Lord. For the husband is the head of the wife as Christ is the head of the church,

his body, of which he is the Savior. Now as the church submits to Christ, so also wives should submit to their husbands in everything.

The husband is the head of the wife and is to lead her in everything. Now, you tell me. Whose job is it to lead in these couple times? It's your job, husband. It's a tough job, but you can do it.

Husband, I want you to lead in three ways. First, you're in charge of scheduling at least four talk times per week. Second, make sure the talk times really happen. Tell your wife when it's time to sit down. Third, guide the content and flow of the talk times. You will ensure that certain progressive steps are completed in each talk time.

You're thinking, "What progressive steps?" I'm about to tell you.

Do the Three-Step

In this first week of the program, I want you to follow these three steps—in order—during each of your four to seven couple times.

First: Start with a Brief Prayer

Husband, take your wife's hand and say a short prayer. Use words like these: "Father, thank you for our marriage. Thank you for this time together. We need you. Please help each of us to change and change our marriage. Please be with us now, and help us learn to open up and connect in conversation. In Jesus's name, Amen."

That's it! Thirty seconds or fewer. It may be painful or unbelievably awkward, but this brief prayer will make a difference.

Prayer will connect you. Prayer creates a deeper mood and makes it easier to talk. Prayer will soften your hearts. Prayer will remind you of God's love and presence and power.

And most important of all, God will answer your brief prayer! He *will* help you open up and talk. He *will* help you change your marriage. He loves you, and he loves your marriage. When he's asked to help change it, that's exactly what he'll do. "If any of you lacks wisdom, he should ask God, who gives generously to all without finding fault, and it will be given to him" (James 1:5).

It won't change overnight, but it will through the 90-day process.

Second: Read Your Couple's Devotional

Husband, read a page from a couple's devotional. Then, both of you answer the questions at the end of the page. This is an easy way to warm up and get a conversation started. I suggest *Night Light: A Devotional for Couples* by James and Shirley Dobson, or *Moments Together for Couples*, by Dennis and Barbara Rainey.

Third: "What's on Your Mind?"

In this step, you each bring up topics connected to your personal lives: work, family and friends, what happened today or yesterday, your spiritual life, church, stresses and worries, and events that triggered strong emotions. You're sharing what's going on in your lives and your honest feelings about these things. Just as you'd do with a friend over lunch. You are sharing yourself as you really are—not what you want to be or how you want others to see you, but the real you. This might be a little frightening at first.

For this first week, and several more weeks to come, avoid conflict completely. Don't even bring up any sensitive topic that might lead to a conflict. If you slip and an argument or disagreement erupts, shut it down immediately. You're not ready for conflict, so you'll do more damage with your old dysfunctional fighting pattern. In Week 6, I'll teach you how to resolve conflicts in a healthy way.

Beginning with Week 2, you will be using this "What's on Your Mind?" step to do your Change Your Marriage Homework assignments.

These couple times won't be a lot of fun for a while. They will be strained. Weird. Extremely uncomfortable. You'll each think of a million reasons not to do them. That's normal, because your marriage is a mess. You may think it won't help, that your situation is hopeless, and that you don't want to spend time together. *Do your Couple Talk Times anyway.* And keep on doing them. Trust me, these talk times will not only play a huge part in healing your marriage, but they will also end up being the centerpiece of your new, vibrant, and intimate marriage.

Homework: Week 1

1. Begin working to improve your personal relationship with God:
   - Have a daily time with God, including prayer and reading the Bible and meditating on it.
   - Attend a local church weekly with the family and get involved in a Sunday morning Bible class, a Bible study, or another small group.
   - Begin a relationship with God through his Son, Jesus, if you have never established this relationship by inviting Jesus into your heart and life.
2. Begin praying and looking for one same-sex accountability partner. When you find one, ask this person to support you as you work on the Change Your Marriage steps. Meet once a week in person and keep in contact by telephone.
3. Have at least four twenty-to-thirty-minute Couple Talk Times each week. Shoot for seven and get at least four. With the husband leading, follow the three steps: Brief Prayer, Couple's Devotional, and "What's on Your Mind?"

3

"I'm Wrong, I'm Sorry, I'll Change"

In the second year of my psychology graduate program at Western Conservative Baptist Seminary, I took a group therapy class. I'll never forget the experience. There were twelve of us in the class. For the first three weeks, Dr. Wayne Colwell lectured on the theory and practice of group therapy. I assumed the entire semester would be the standard lecture format. Oh, how wrong I was.

When we entered the classroom at the beginning of the fourth week, there were thirteen chairs arranged in a circle. Dr. Colwell, with a little smirk on his face, sat in one of the chairs. When we had all taken our seats, Dr. Colwell said, "No more lectures. No more theory. It's time to actually do group therapy." For the rest of the semester, with Dr. Colwell as group leader, that's what we did.

Everyone took turns being on the hot seat. I thoroughly enjoyed watching each of my classmates take their turn under the microscope. I gave advice, pointed out personality quirks and flaws, and tried to help each person make healthy changes. I thought group therapy was great fun.

Then it was my turn, and the fun stopped. Suddenly, *I* was the one on the hot seat. Twelve pairs of eyes were on me. It wasn't the eyes that bothered me. It was the twelve mouths and what they said about me. My fellow graduate students, with whom I had worked and studied and laughed for over a year, picked me apart. My classmates made me face the real me. The guy who didn't reveal much of himself. Who didn't allow others to get too close. Who made a joke when the conversation got a little too deep or personal.

I didn't like being a bug under glass back in 1985. It was painful. But I learned a lot about myself during my hot seat experience. I talked to Sandy about what happened and took some steps that have greatly improved my marriage and relationships with others. I can honestly say that group session changed my life.

My group therapy experience led to real changes in me. Why? Because I was forced to look in the mirror and admit my faults. I wasn't allowed to run and hide from the unflattering truth about me and the mistakes I was making in my relationships.

An essential part of the marital change process is identifying your faults in the relationship and working to correct them.

"It's Not My Fault!"

Sandy and I have four children: Emily, Leeann, Nancy, and William. As they grew up, they had plenty of sibling rivalry. Over the years, they had countless petty squabbles and fights. If two of them were in the same vicinity for more than three minutes, a battle of some kind would erupt.

I don't know how many times I rushed to the scene of a conflict between two of them. I don't know why I even bothered, but I'd ask, "What happened?" Always—and I mean always—I'd be treated to the same responses: "She did it!" "He did it!" "It was her fault!" "I didn't do anything!" "I only did what I did because he did what he did!" "It's not my fault!"

Just once I wanted to hear one of my kids admit fault. Just once! "Okay, Dad, it was my fault. I called her a mean name and stole her toy. I'm sorry, and I'm ready to take my punishment." As all you fellow parents know, I never heard words like these.

Some Things Never Change

The sad truth is, adults in a marriage are no different from two kids locked in a conflict. It's never your fault, is it? It's always your spouse's fault, isn't it? When something goes wrong in your marriage, you blame each other. I know you do, because I've been guilty of the same thing in my marriage. My first reaction is to blame Sandy. And her first reaction is to blame me. It's what we all tend to do. It's not right. It's not godly. But it's human nature.

As the difficulties in a marriage deepen, this focus on the other partner's faults becomes more intense, entrenched, and intractable.

I have witnessed the same old "It's not my fault" scenario in nearly every first session with the married couples I've seen in therapy. After taking a brief history of each spouse, I ask, "What brings you in today?" Over the next twenty to thirty minutes, each spouse blames the other for their marriage problems:

"He never talks."   "He won't do any chores."
"She never stops talking."   "She's too focused on the kids."
"He works too many hours."   "He's not affectionate."
"She doesn't keep the house   "She doesn't respect me."
clean."   "He's not romantic."
"He's lazy."

"She won't have sex with me." "He won't be the spiritual
"He hates my family."   leader."
"She spends too much."   "She won't let me parent the
                                stepkids."

And on and on and on. I'm going to tell you the same
thing I tell these married couples: "Stop looking at your
spouse's faults. You're probably right about the faults, but
it doesn't do any good to focus on them. Who cares? Focusing
on your spouse's weaknesses and mistakes will never lead to
any change in your marriage. I want you to do something
very difficult but vitally important. I want you to look in the
mirror. I want you to focus on your faults."

Let's say I asked you—right now—to list your spouse's
faults in the marriage. You'd have no problem doing it, would
you? You'd reel off a long litany of faults in record time.
And you'd be correct. I mean, you ought to know, you live
with this person. Too bad it would be a complete waste of
time. Actually, it would be worse than that. Focusing on your
partner's faults keeps your marriage stuck and in trouble and
joyless and fun-less. As long as you keep the spotlight on your
spouse and what's wrong with him or her, no improvement
of any kind can take place in your relationship.

It's a Mexican Standoff

When you focus on the faults of your spouse, you're being
selfish. Selfishness is the opposite of true biblical love. In
God's plan for marriage, meeting your spouse's needs is your
number one priority (1 Cor. 13:4–7; Eph. 5:22–33; 1 Peter
3:1–7). Each of you has deep, God-ordained male and female
needs that only a husband and wife can fill; if you don't fill
your partner's needs, those vital needs go unmet. And that
leaves that person out in the cold—literally.

Selfishness is the root cause of most marital problems. A selfish spouse sees no need to change. "Our problems are your fault. I'm not perfect, but my mistakes aren't as bad as yours. When you change, our marriage will get better."

The driving force behind selfishness is a desperate desire to protect yourself. You are trying to avoid the pain of facing and working on *your* faults. Ironically, your pain increases because your selfishness prevents any improvement in your marriage. As your marriage falters and you slowly kill it, at least you have the satisfaction of knowing it's not your fault. But the cost is huge and will last a lifetime.

When you focus on the faults of your spouse, you force your spouse into a defensive reaction. Have you ever gotten this kind of response after you attempt to pin most of the blame on your spouse for a marital problem: "Wow, you really called me on the carpet. You're right, this is all my fault. I'll do my best to change, starting right now."

Maybe in your dreams. But never in real life. You know what happens. Your spouse bristles with anger, rears up, and fires back at you, "Oh yeah? Well, let me tell you about your faults, O perfect one!" You are hit with a stream of *your* blunders.

It's a Mexican standoff. Both of you focusing on the faults of the other. Neither one willing to budge. This blame-it-on-your-spouse strategy began with the first couple on earth. When God asked Adam if he had eaten from the forbidden fruit tree in the Garden of Eden, Adam replied:

> The woman you put here with me—she gave me some fruit from the tree, and I ate it.
>
> Genesis 3:12

Adam's attempt to shift the blame to Eve didn't work. The truth is, they *both* sinned. Blaming your spouse will only make your marriage worse. You and your spouse are both responsible for the condition of your marriage. Therefore, each of you must identify your mistakes and bad behavior and work to change. You must focus on the only person in the universe you can change: you!

In marriages in which only one spouse has sinned seriously (adultery, pornography, alcoholism, drug addiction, physical and verbal abuse, etc.), that must be dealt with first and in special ways. The sinning spouse must repent, show real change, and help his or her spouse heal from the trauma of the sinful behavior. Then, and only then, the other spouse will focus on his or her mistakes in the marriage. I explain this process in Chapters 17, 18, and 19.

Whatever Happened to Repentance?

The next step in the Change Your Marriage program requires you and your spouse to go through a process of repentance together. These days no one seems to know how to correctly repent. When actors, athletes, and politicians are caught in sinful behavior, their apologies are often incredibly weak and watered down and self-serving:

"I made a mistake."
"If my behavior offended anyone . . ."
"I haven't done anything wrong."
"I'm guilty of poor judgment, a misstep. . . ."
"I have an addiction" (in which case a plan for recovery is essential).
"I got some bad advice."

Lame. Very lame. Their poor apologies, which aren't apologies at all, make matters worse. It's obvious these public figures aren't sorry for what they've done. It's obvious they are not admitting the entire truth. It's obvious they're not going to change their behavior.

True, biblical repentance is a key link in the change process. The New Testament word translated repentance is *metanoia*,

43

and it is "a turning from (sin)" and "a turning to" a new path, to faith in Christ. It contains four elements:

1. Confessing your sin in a specific, detailed way ("I did this. . . . It was wrong."). It means saying the same thing about your sins that God does (1 John 1:9).
2. Feeling sorry and realizing the impact your sin has had on God and others
3. Asking for forgiveness
4. Changing your behavior (making a 180-degree turn)

A great example of biblical repentance is the story of King David's sin with Bathsheba (2 Samuel 11–12) and his confession of that sin (Psalm 51). Read these passages and you will see and feel real repentance from a man after God's own heart (1 Sam. 13:14), who sinned grievously.

What God wants in your repentance is godly sorrow. This kind of sorrow means being broken and humbled; it is prompted by God, not self. In 2 Corinthians 7:9–11, Paul teaches this progression: godly sorrow leads to repentance, which leads to changed behavior. What Paul is talking about in this passage is *genuine heart change*.

In confessing and repenting before God, David spoke these words to God:

> The sacrifices of God are a broken spirit;
> a broken and contrite heart,
> O God, you will not despise.
>
> Psalm 51:17

The Letter of Responsibility

Your job in Week 2 is to sit down and write what I call the Letter of Responsibility. It's a letter to your spouse containing all *your* mistakes from the day you met to today. It must be a full-fledged *letter*, with sentences and paragraphs. You don't confess your mistakes with a list or with a set of bullet points. Your letter must explain each bad behavior, without any qualifications or excuses or rationalizations.

This is a carefully written letter of repentance that will take time to complete. You will think hard about it. You will pray that God will reveal the mistakes you've made and the mistakes you continue to make in your marriage. It will take at least three to four days to finish. You have one full week—seven days—to complete it. You will write it on your own, with no input from your spouse or anyone else.

Your Letter of Responsibility will include the four elements of repentance as noted on the preceding page.

1. Confessing Your Sin in a Specific, Detailed Way

Your letter will not be a general "I'm sorry for all my mistakes," paint-with-a-broad-brush message. It will be a detailed account, as specific as you can make it, of what you believe you've done wrong or what has obviously offended, hurt, or caused sadness to your spouse in the relationship. The more specific the better. The longer the letter the better. You will include past mistakes that you have not repeated and current bad actions. Typically, many of your mistakes will be chronic patterns of behavior in which you have engaged for years.

When you mention a mistake, give examples to be clear and to convince your spouse that you do understand what you've done wrong. If you've been selfish, write out some stories of your selfishness:

"I've refused to do the laundry."

"I denied you sex many times."

"When conflict occurs, I walk away."

"I missed your office party because I was watching a ball game."

"I bought sports equipment for myself while complaining to you about your use of money."

"I seldom if ever praised you for what you do for me—like working hard at your job, cooking meals, romancing me."

You obviously can't put on paper all the mistakes you've made. There isn't that much paper. Don't hesitate to include gross mistakes in addition to minor offenses. Tell the whole truth. Just do the best, most thorough job possible. If in doubt, write more. It's better if your letter is too long than too short. Since it is part of a healthy, healing process, each of you won't mind reading a long letter.

2. Feeling Sorry and Realizing the Impact Your Sin Has Had on Your Spouse

It's important to communicate that you feel bad for the mistakes you've made. You know you've caused pain in your partner, and you are making a sincere attempt to feel some of his or her pain. In other words, you are truly trying to walk in your spouse's shoes and trying to feel what he or she felt as a result of your mistakes, your lack of love, the offenses you committed.

As you describe each of your misdeeds, identify the emotion you think that action triggered in your partner. "I'm sorry for all my long hours at work and for neglecting you. My selfish workaholism must have made you feel angry, hurt, and rejected."

This kind of empathy will build a bridge—a small, shaky bridge, but a bridge nevertheless—between the two of you. Your spouse will believe that you "get it," that you understand the damage your behavior has caused. Therefore, the intensity of your spouse's resentments will be reduced.

Admit that your mistakes in your marriage are ultimately disobedience toward God. The sin of failing to love and care for your spouse is first a sin against God. King David acknowledged this: "Against you, you only, have I sinned" (Ps. 51:4). You have sinned because you have disobeyed God's commands to you as a husband and a wife. Acknowledging that you have grieved God is part of repentance and will motivate you to improve your behavior.

3. Asking for Forgiveness

Failure to humbly ask for forgiveness indicates that you aren't truly sorry for what you have contributed to the harm done your marriage. Not asking for forgiveness, from God and from your spouse, means you do not consider your behavior as really serious. You are protecting yourself and being arrogant. You don't "get it."

So after describing each mistake, ask for the forgiveness of God and of your spouse for that poor or harmful behavior. God will forgive you immediately (1 John 1:9) and "will remember [your] sins no more" (Jer. 31:34). It will take longer for your spouse to forgive, but your request for forgiveness aids the process.

4. Changing Your Behavior

Repentance is not complete until behavior is changed—new actions initiated and old harmful ones stopped. Words are nice, but they mean nothing if not put into action. In fact, if you fail to act, you are a liar and your expressions of confession and repentance are a dysfunctional joke. If you follow my instructions but fail to change, your lack of changed behavior will seriously discourage your spouse and cause even more damage to your marriage.

It's better to not even pretend to repent than to mouth words of confession and sorrow and repentance with no corresponding change in your behavior.

The final section of your Letter of Responsibility contains specific promises of new behavior. You mention again each improper or neglectful or harmful thing you have done and write how you will aggressively correct it. You communicate exactly what you will do to address those things you have done that are damaging to the marriage and what you will do to act differently:

> "I know I've been a workaholic; I will talk to my boss about reducing my hours and be home by 6:30 p.m. each night."
>
> "I've been very critical of you; I give you permission to tell me when I'm being critical. And I will praise you at least once a day for a behavior of yours or for a character trait or for one of the thousands of things you do for me and for the children."

"I have been a lazy slug when I get home from work. I will ask you each evening what jobs I can do for you."

"I will show some warmth when you kiss me."

Your Letters of Responsibility will lead to a better balance in your marriage. You've *both* made mistakes. You've both played a part in messing up your relationship and short-circuiting the fun and happiness and fulfillment you started with. It naturally follows that you both must play a part in repairing your relationship.

These letters will also generate some much needed humility, understanding, and mutual respect. Plus, in them you will have identified a number of specific areas of weakness you each need to change.

I understand that these letters will be very difficult to accomplish, particularly if your marriage is in serious turmoil. What I'm asking you to do, to truly repent in these four specific areas and humbly address your faults, is exactly the opposite of what you feel like doing. I know that.

Your letters won't be the most heartfelt, genuine expressions of repentance ever written. Just do your best, with God's help, to set aside your resentments toward your spouse and focus on you and your mistakes. Ask God to give you that "mustard seed" of faith to do this assignment. That will be enough.

Read Your Letters

On day seven of Week 2 (or before), sit down together and read your Letters of Responsibility out loud to one another. The husband schedules the meeting and makes sure it happens. Carve out at least two hours for this meeting. Use a private, quiet place in your home where there will be no distractions. Your children should be asleep or confined to their rooms. No one but the two of you should hear your letters.

The husband prays briefly before the readings. Ask God to bless what you're about to do and to use it to promote change in your marriage. Then the husband reads his letter. If she feels led to do it, the wife thanks him for the letter and mentions the parts of it that particularly impressed her or touched her in a positive way.

After the wife has given her positive responses (are you getting the impression you need to be positive?), she reads her letter. The husband listens and gives his responses.

No negative comments are allowed. Don't say anything that would take away from the value of your spouse's honest effort to confess and repent.

Just listen attentively and politely, and make positive, accepting, encouraging statements.

Week 3

Do the Top Two

Immediately following the readings and the responses, you need to move into action mode. God wants change to begin right away, so Week 3 starts with each spouse identifying his or her Top Two Mistakes and coming up with a plan to correct those mistakes.

The husband, going first again as the leader, asks his wife to tell him what Top Two Mistakes she wants him to work on in the next week. Her Top Two Mistakes will probably be from his Letter of Responsibility. But they could be mistakes he did not include in his letter.

Your Top Two need to be behaviors that are small but important and that can be done every day. By small, I mean attainable. Don't choose a huge area of weakness for your spouse to tackle. A behavior that can be done daily will create momentum and hope in your relationship.

The wife identifies her Top Two and clearly explains the specific behaviors her husband can do to correct each mistake. As she tells him her Top Two and the how-tos, he writes on a 3x5 index card what he needs to do for her happiness.

One Husband's Top Two Index Card

1. Not doing enough chores around the home
   How-to: Within five minutes of arriving home, I will ask Betty what chore I can do for her. Then I'll do that chore in her time frame.
2. Lack of affection
   How-to: A decent kiss and hug before I leave for work and right when I get home. If my kiss and hug aren't affectionate enough, she'll tell me, and I will repeat until acceptable.

When the husband has filled out his index card, it's the wife's turn to ask him to identify her Top Two Mistakes and how she can correct these mistakes every day.

Use part of your Couple Talk Time during Week 3 to discuss your progress in correcting your Top Two Mistakes. Ask your spouse how you're doing and use that input to make changes and adjustments. If you discover you have bitten off more than you can chew and you're not ready or able to do a certain behavior, admit this to your spouse and switch to a different behavior.

The Payoffs

The action steps for Weeks 2 and 3, the Letters of Responsibility and the Top Two, are expressions of your obedience to God. They show you are working toward repentance and change. They soften your hearts. They put the focus where it belongs: on *you* and what *you* can do to improve the marriage. They create change. Not a massive change, but a little change; and any change is a good thing. They help put into place a vital component of your new, healthy marriage: always adjusting to meet the real needs of your spouse.

I've told you what you need to do in Weeks 2 and 3. Now I'm going to show you how it looks in the life of a married couple. Your homework is found at the end of Chapter 4.

4

Where the Rubber Meets the Road

One Couple's Journey
through Weeks 2 and 3

It's my second session with Steve and Sharon. We discuss the progress they've made on their Week 1 assignments: grow spiritually, find an accountability partner, and establish regular Couple Talk Times.

I explain their Week 2 assignment: the Letter of Responsibility. I tell them: "One week from now, when you've read your letters, you'll know exactly why your marriage has broken down. The causes will be crystal clear."

Here are the letters they read out loud in my therapy office. Reading them will show you how to do this assignment. Unless you're seeing a therapist, you'll need to read your letters at home.

Steve's Letter of Responsibility

Dear Sharon,
As I thought and prayed about doing this letter, it became clear how many mistakes I've made as your

husband. There are so many that I can't possibly put them all in one letter. But I will do my best to cover all my serious, major mistakes. I want you to know two things before I begin describing my mistakes.

First, I have committed these marital sins not only against you. I've come to realize that I have sinned against God by mistreating you. I have broken God's commands to me as a husband. So I'm asking both God and you to forgive me.

Second, my poor behavior is 100 percent my fault. You had nothing to do with any of my mistakes as your husband. I am the one to blame for what I have done wrong in our relationship. I've blamed you many times for my behavior, and I've been wrong to do that. I guess that's my first mistake!

I want to go over mistakes I've made in the past before I get to the more current, ongoing patterns of bad behavior. Back when we were dating, I made the terrible mistake of staying in contact with my ex-girlfriend. For about three months I talked on the phone with her about once a week and even went to lunch with her twice. There were five or six emails back and forth, too. Stupid, stupid, stupid. And wrong. And very hurtful to you. When you found out, you were devastated.

I am so sorry for betraying you this way. I was insecure and still had feelings for her. But there is no excuse. It was wrong and I should never have done it. I know we talked about it back then, but I want to mention it here because it was such a big mistake. It hurt you badly and made you wonder about my love and commitment to you. I don't blame you for wondering. I'm sorry and I ask you to forgive me.

In the first ten years of our marriage, I made some important decisions without your input. Going on vacation with my parents. Changing jobs. Making those mutual fund investments. I wanted to make those decisions without any interference from you. I knew what I wanted to do, and I didn't want to deal with your objections. I was wrong. I was wrong and selfish and controlling. I made you feel small, insignificant, and not needed. You must have felt angry, humiliated, and betrayed. I'm sorry for cutting you out of those decisions. Please forgive me. You are my partner, and we need to discuss all decisions together, pray about them together, and make them together.

Now to my current mistakes. The first thing that jumps out at me is that I have not been the spiritual leader in our marriage. According to the Bible, that's my job. And I've blown it, year after year. I'll improve for a few weeks, then stop again. We haven't prayed together much. We haven't read the Bible or a couple's devotional. We rarely talk about our spiritual lives. I'm sorry for dropping the ball in this critically important area. I know it's hurt our relationship and kept us from being closer. It's also hurt your respect for me. Please forgive me for not leading you (and the kids) spiritually.

I have not made time to sit down with you and have conversations with you. Like my dad, I hold a lot inside and I don't talk personally. But I want a better marriage than my parents have had, so I need to start talking with you more. I've kept my personal thoughts and feelings to myself. You've been frustrated, very hurt, and lonely. These talk times Dr. Clarke has us doing will help. I'm sorry for not talking and making time with you. Will you forgive me?

I'm a workaholic. I have, many times, put my career ahead of you and the kids. The late hours, the phone calls and emails at home, answering my dumb cell phone when I'm with you, the broken promises, missing dates and special family activities because of work . . . I've done them all, way too many times. You are more

*important—way more important—than my job, and I
need to prove it. I'm sorry for not making you and the
kids a priority. I know you have resented me and felt
unloved and not valuable because of my workaholism.
I'm sorry for this selfish behavior. Please forgive me.*

*I've also been lousy at doing my share of the chores.
For years, I figured I worked hard enough at my job
and shouldn't have to do much around the house.
Wrong. I've been totally wrong and insensitive. I've
avoided doing chores all kinds of ways: ignoring your
requests, agreeing to do chores and then not following
through, forgetting to do chores, making the kids do
them, only doing the chores I wanted to do. You've
had to work harder and longer in the home because
of my laziness. You've felt devalued and tired and
resentful. You've felt like my maid and housekeeper,
not my life partner. I'm sorry for not doing my share
of the chores and home duties. These aren't just your
jobs that I'm helping you with. These jobs are my jobs,
too. Please forgive me and let me show you a different
husband.*

*Okay, now it's time to tell you what I plan to do
differently in these areas of weakness. I know words are
cheap and I have to actually do what I say I'm going to
do.*

*Let me handle the past mistakes first. Since you
found out about my contact with my ex, I have had no
contact with her and I never will. You are my woman
and there is no one else. Regarding decisions, we have
done pretty well as a team the last number of years.
I commit that I will continue to talk with you about
every key decision we face. Not just talk and discuss
but also pray about these decisions.*

*In the area of spiritual leadership in our home, I will
pray with you briefly and read a couple's devotional at
every Couple Talk Time. We did this at our four Talk*

Times this past week and it felt good. Did you like it? I know it's not much, but it's a start. As we continue in the 90-Day Program, I hope to do more with you in the spiritual area. It's my job to make sure we grow closer spiritually. I also want to lead the family in a once-a-week devotion time, but I don't feel ready to do this yet. Once you and I are doing better as a couple, we'll talk about the family spiritual time and we'll start doing it.

I commit to you to work hard to share more personally with you. In each Couple Talk Time, I will share at least one personal item with you: a thought, an emotion, something spiritual, etc. I know it won't be too impressive at first, but I will learn and get better at letting you see the real, inside me.

I will do three things to reduce my workaholism. One, I will talk with my boss this week and tell him I'm a workaholic and that I'm going to make some changes for my wife and kids. Two, I will try to be home at 6:00 p.m. each evening. If I'll be later than 6:00 p.m., I will call you and let you know. Three, I will not answer my cell phone at home. I will also not do work emails at home unless it's very important, and only after dinner, after my time with you, and after my time with the kids.

With household chores, I will sit down with you this next week and get a list of regular chores you want me to do each week. I'll post my list on the fridge and follow through. If I miss a posted chore, you have my permission to remind me. Also, within fifteen minutes of getting home each evening from work, I'll ask you what one chore I can do for you around the home.

Sharon, the honest truth is I don't feel like making these changes. We're not close now and our marriage is in trouble. But I can't let feelings control my behavior toward you. I've done that throughout our marriage. I

will work to make these changes because God wants me
to and because I know they will help heal our marriage.
Love,
Steve

Sharon's Letter of Responsibility

Dear Steve:
This was a hard letter to write. I couldn't seem to get
started. Truth is, I have been focused on your mistakes
and could not see my own. It dawned on me that it's
impossible for all our marriage problems to be your
fault. You get half the blame and I get half the blame.
So here's my half.

For the first eight or so years of our marriage, I
overspent. I bought things for myself, the kids, and
the home that we didn't need. I was a shopaholic.
Shopping and buying was a way for me to handle stress
and feel happy. Of course, it ended up just making
me—and you—miserable. Oh, the fights we had over
my spending! I tried to justify what I bought, and I kept
on spending.

Steve, I put way too much financial pressure on you.
I wasted a lot of money for my own selfish reasons. I
had a problem and I refused to admit it. I'm sorry for
the pain and anguish my spending caused you. Please
forgive me for all my spending mistakes. It was sin and I
know that now.

Until about five years ago, my temper was a real
problem. In our conflicts, I'd escalate quickly and
start yelling and screaming at you. I said many mean,
sarcastic, and belittling things to you. I couldn't control
my emotional intensity, like my dad, but there's no
excuse. I hurt you over and over again with my mouth.
I'm sure you felt angry, very hurt, less of a man. I

*disrespected you and I'm very sorry for my verbal abuse
of you. Yes, it was verbal abuse. I've gotten a lot better in
recent years, but I did a lot of damage. Please forgive me.*

Here are some big mistakes I continue to make.

*First, I have not been a good sexual partner for
you. I know physical affection, touch, and sex are very
important to you, but I've done a lousy job meeting
your needs in this area. I have selfishly denied you
physically many, many times. I don't need touch and
sex as much as you do, so I've only been as physical as I
wanted to be. That is sin because it's selfish and fails to
meet your needs.*

*You touch me in affectionate ways a lot, but I rarely
touch you unless we're having sex. Speaking of sex, I've
said no to you way too much. I knew my rejection hurt
you, but I didn't care. Even if I was resentful or angry
with you about something else, I should have talked it
out so we could then make love.*

*I can't imagine how rejected and sexually frustrated
I've made you over the years. I kept my body away from
you, and that was not my right to do. I'm sorry for
treating you this way. Please forgive me.*

*Second, I have made the mistake of spending too
much time and energy on the kids and the home.
Having the kids' needs met and our home clean and
organized means more to me than you do. You ask me
for something, ask me to take a walk, ask me to go out
on a date, ask me for sex . . . and too often I've said no
because of the kids or household jobs.*

*After doing things for the kids and doing all the
chores, I'm too tired to do anything with you. That's
insulting and wrong. You must feel angry, hurt, and way
down on my list of priorities. Steve, I'm sorry for this
behavior. Please forgive me.*

*Third, I'm a nag and I know it. My mom was very
critical as I grew up, so I guess that's where I learned the*

fine art of nagging and negativity. But it's not my mom's fault. It's my fault. I criticize you often and point out what you don't do. I don't praise you very often for all the things you do for me and the kids.

My nagging has made you feel defensive, henpecked, and like a failure. You probably think you can't do anything to please me. That you're never good enough for me. I'm sorry for my critical, negative comments. I sincerely hope you will forgive me.

Finally, Steve, I don't do many couple activities you want to do. You have asked me many times to sit by you and watch a show or a ball game on television, play golf or tennis with you, take a walk or a bike ride, or get breakfast together on a Saturday morning. I always say no—too busy, too tired, don't feel like it. . . . I have hurt you and robbed you of many chances to build our relationship.

I want to sit down and talk with you—and that's important—but I see the activities you want to do with me as silly and not important. I am wrong, I have hurt you, and I'm sorry. Please forgive me.

Steve, I've not been the wife God wants me to be for you. I've made a lot of mistakes. I certainly haven't covered them all in this letter, but these are what I see as the worst and most damaging.

I don't feel as if I can make big changes yet, but I want to begin to make some small changes. Here is what I plan to do to correct my mistakes.

I think I've done well on my overspending and verbal attacks on you. We work well together on our budget and talk about what we can and can't afford. I know I still yell, but it's rare and I can stop it pretty fast. I commit to keep on making progress in these two areas.

Physically, I'm not ready for serious kissing or making out or sex. I'm too hurt and I just can't go too far physically yet. What I want to do is give you a ten-

*minute neck or foot massage four days a week. You can
ask for the massage at any time during these four days,
but I have a suggestion: I'll do the massage before each
of our four Couple Talk Times. That way, it'll be easy
to remember, and it also may increase our closeness
during the Talk Times.*

*Regarding the kids and the home, I will get the
kids to bed each night at 8:30. Then, I will offer to do
something with you for the next thirty minutes. It could
be one of our Couple Talk Times or something else you
want to do. After the thirty minutes, I'll do any chores
that still need to be done.*

*I will learn to praise you a lot more often. I will give
you one compliment per day. It might be praise for a
character trait, your work ethic, a spiritual quality, or
something you've done for me.*

*As for activities with just the two of us, I think my
offer of thirty minutes at 8:30 daily will help correct
this mistake. If you want and need extra time, maybe
we could do an activity together on a Saturday once
a month. Something that might take several hours or
more. I'll do any activity—except bowling—that you
want to do.*

*Steve, I'm praying that God will give me the strength
and motivation to follow through on these promised
changes. I can't do these on my own. I believe he will
help me because he wants our marriage to get healthy.*

Love,
Sharon

The Mystery Is Solved

Can you see why Steve and Sharon's marriage is in trouble?
It's no mystery. Their Letters of Responsibility reveal the
mistakes that killed their love and ruined their marriage. Your

Letters of Responsibility will do the same for you and your spouse. They will reveal the specific causes of your marriage problems, the mistakes you each have made over the course of your relationship.

The positive steps you take to correct these mistakes will reverse the deterioration of your love and significantly aid in the improvement of your marriage. Your Letters of Responsibility are a blueprint for the successful restoration of your relationship!

Realistically, I know and you know that you can't change all these areas of weakness overnight. But you can start small changes overnight. The small changes will lead to big changes and to a brand-new marriage.

I want you to hang on to the Letters of Responsibility you wrote and read to one another. Keep them as a written reminder of the small changes you have committed to do. But for the time being—at least the next week—you will be working to correct only your Top Two mistakes.

All the mistakes and corrective changes in your Letters of Responsibility will be highlighted several weeks down the road in your 90-day program.

Steve and Sharon's Top Two

After Steve and Sharon read their Letters of Responsibility and gave positive feedback to each other for what they wrote, I explained the Top Two assignment they would accomplish in the next week (Week 3). With Steve going first, they asked each other what Top Two mistakes they needed to change in the next week.

Steve and Sharon's Top Two came directly from their Letters. The key addition was that they had to carry out each behavior every day.

Here are their Top Two, written on index cards.

Steve's Top Two

1. Not sharing enough personal information

   How-to: I will share at least one personal item with Sharon every day: a thought, an emotion, something spiritual, etc.

2. Not doing enough chores around the house

   How-to: Within fifteen minutes of arriving home from work, Monday through Friday, I will ask what chore I can do for Sharon. On Saturday and Sunday, I will ask for one chore before 5:00 p.m.

Sharon's Top Two

1. Not being physically affectionate

   How-to: I will give Steve a ten-minute neck or foot massage every day. I will do four of the massages before our couple talk times. On the other three days, I will bring up the massage topic and ask Steve when he wants me to do it.

2. Not praising Steve enough

   How-to: I will give Steve one compliment per day: a character trait, his work ethic, a spiritual quality, or something he's done for me.

Steve and Sharon used part of each Couple Talk Time during Week 3 to evaluate their progress in correcting their Top Two mistakes. Neither one had a perfect record for the week, but they did enough positive, corrective behaviors to breathe some much-needed life into their relationship.

They were a little closer to changing their marriage.

Homework: Weeks 2 and 3

1. Continue to improve your personal relationship with God, stay in contact with your accountability partner, and have your four Couple Talk Times.
2. Each read, alone, 2 Samuel 11–12 and Psalm 51. Use part of your Couple Talk Time to discuss what these passages communicate about true repentance.
3. Within seven days, each of you write your Letter of Responsibility. Include the four elements of repentance:
   • Confess your sins in a specific, detailed way, owning complete responsibility for them.
   • Ask God for true feelings of sorrow for your sin, and express these feelings. Try honestly and diligently to comprehend the impact your sin has had on God and on your spouse.
   • Ask for forgiveness.
   • Change your behavior.
4. Read your Letters of Responsibility. Each of you makes positive comments about your spouse's Letter.
5. Put your Top Two mistakes and how to correct them on an index card. During Week 3, do your daily corrective behaviors, and in your Couple Talk Times, get updates on your progress from your spouse.

5

A Breath of Fresh, Positive Air

I have a few quirks. All right, I have more than a few quirks. In fact, *quirks* is a nice way of describing my many incredibly annoying habits. Here's a sample of the kind of irritating behaviors Sandy has to deal with on a daily basis.

Food

I go on and off food items. Suddenly and unpredictably, I decide I don't like a particular dish that Sandy has cooked and put on the table. I'll take a bite and say, "I'm off that. I can't eat it."

Unfortunately, I don't know I'm off a certain food until I eat it. Sandy has told me many times that it would be helpful to know *ahead of time* that I don't want a particular dish. I'm sure it would be helpful, but I have no control over my on-and-off food system.

The period of time I stay off a food varies greatly. It might be a few days or a few years. Once, after I had eaten and enjoyed it for the first twenty years of our marriage, I went off steak for a year and a half! Then, one day, out of the blue, I realized I was ready to eat steak again. I couldn't explain it to Sandy. I just knew I wanted to resume eating steak.

Also, I have a chronic habit of never finishing a container of food or drink. I'll always leave a small amount of a leftover dish behind. one scoop of casserole, one or two tater tots, three green beans, the smallest sliver of pie. . . . The next family member takes the container out of the refrigerator, thinking there's a reasonable amount of food left in it, and discovers there's only a tiny fraction in there.

I'll leave one or two swallows of milk or iced tea behind. The worst offense is when I leave one cookie in the cookie tin. Now, that's cruel. Who wants to eat just one cookie?

I know this behavior of leaving miniscule amounts of food behind is wrong. And selfish. But I can't stop it. They don't have rehab centers for this kind of addiction.

Driving

I drive like a maniac. I always have. My mother has a lead foot, so maybe it's her fault. To me, every car trip is a NASCAR race and I drive to win. A yellow light means *gun it, you can make it through that light!* I drive aggressively, weave in and out of traffic, and honk my horn frequently.

I honk at fellow motorists for going too slowly. For going too fast. For not immediately accelerating when a light turns green. For not pushing out and turning left on a yellow light. For not using turn signals. For having an ugly car. For having a beautiful, sleek sports car that I envy. I don't at honk school buses, nuns, and motorists with Christian symbols on their vehicles.

The other day, I actually honked at a police officer for not taking off fast enough when a light turned green. That honk wasn't a good idea.

How Does Sandy Do It?

This is just a partial list of my many quirks. I snore, too. Do you get the impression it can be pretty difficult to live with me? How does Sandy deal with all my annoying, negative qualities? I'll tell you how. By focusing on my many *positive qualities*. I'd list my positive qualities, but it would take five or six chapters.

In healthy marriages, spouses focus on each other's positives. In unhealthy, struggling marriages, spouses focus on each other's negatives. That's what is happening in your marriage, isn't it? All you can see are the negatives about each other. Your daily dose of negativity is killing your ability to communicate. Your romance. Your love. Your hope.

An essential part of breathing new life and new love into your marriage is forcing yourselves to ignore the negative and pump in the positive.

The Most Positive Couple Who Ever Lived

My beautiful wife, Sandy, and I are the most positive couple who ever lived. Actually, that's not true. We wish! We definitely work at being very positive in our relationship, but we're not number one in positivity. That honor goes to Solomon and Shulamith, the lovers in the Old Testament book of Song of Solomon.

Solomon and Shulamith knew one of the secrets to a happy, intimate marriage: There must be many more positives than negatives in the relationship. Their positives fall into three categories.

First, they did *caring behaviors* for each other. Solomon pursued Shulamith (Song of Songs 2:8–9), he built her self-esteem with praise (1:8–10), and he gently led her in their times of physical intimacy (4:10–5:1). Shulamith gave Solomon respect (1:3), she did fun and playful activities with him outside the home (2:10–13; 7:11–13), and she wanted him physically (1:2–4a; 2:6).

Second, they gave each other *compliments*. Boatloads and boatloads of compliments. Solomon called Shulamith "most beautiful of women" (1:8), "a lily among thorns" (2:2), and "my perfect one" (6:9). Not to be outdone, Shulamith called Solomon "handsome" and "charming" (1:16), "a gazelle or a young stag" (2:9), "outstanding among ten thousand" (5:10).

Third, they *communicated*. I mean, really communicated. Solomon and Shulamith made private time to talk, and they thoroughly enjoyed their conversation (2:3, 14).

Did these positives have an impact on Solomon and Shulamith's relationship? You'd better believe it! They were deeply in love and had passion coming out of their ears. You and your spouse, who have lost most if not all of your love and passion, can begin to get it back by following Solomon and Shulamith's example.

These three positive behaviors worked for them, and they will work for you, too!

The Power of Positivity

As we begin Week 4, I want you to continue the Week 1 pillars: (1) improving your relationship with God, (2) working with your accountability partner, and (3) maintaining four twenty-to-thirty-minute Couple Talk Times per week. Again, you will keep doing these Week 1 behaviors throughout the 90 Days of Change.

The Three Cs

I also want you to force yourselves—and, believe me, you're going to have to force yourselves—to carry out the Three Cs of positivity: (1) caring behaviors, (2) compliments, and (3) communication skills. Week 4 is all about pumping these three positives into your marriage.

Caring Behaviors

Go ahead and get out your Top Two index cards and your Letters of Responsibility. You've just finished doing your Top

Two behaviors every day during Week 3. You're going to continue doing your Top Two every day during Week 4. Also, I want you to add one more mistake and corrective behavior to your Top Two. Follow the same procedure: ask your spouse to choose another mistake from your Letter of Responsibility and jot down on your 3×5 card the mistake and how you will correct it each day.

As before, this extra behavior needs to be small, attainable, and done daily. So, you each will now have a Top Three to do each day during Week 4. These three caring behaviors will produce more positive flow in your relationship.

Using Steve and Sharon again, here are their additional caring behaviors:

Steve's Additional Behavior

3. Not helping put the kids to bed

   How-to: Every night I'm home I will help our son with his bath and pray briefly with each child when he or she is in bed.

Sharon's Additional Behavior

3. Not kissing Steve

   How-to: I will kiss Steve—at least a peck—on the lips once a day.

Compliments

I'll bet there aren't a whole lot of compliments flying around in your relationship. In fact, probably none. When your marriage is struggling and you're unhappy, paying your spouse a compliment is the last thing on your mind. Paying your spouse a critical comment, a sarcastic barb, or an insult comes very easily.

As we saw in Solomon and Shulamith's lives, compliments are always part of a healthy relationship. So to move your marriage toward health, I want you both to go into compliment overdrive during Week 4.

What I'm about to recommend will feel like compliment *overkill* to you. All I can ask is that you trust me and my experience and force yourself to follow my instructions.

You're thinking, "How often am I going to have to compliment my spouse this week?" Here's my answer: Lay two compliments a day on your spouse. Preferably, one in the morning and one later in the day. These compliments need to be delivered verbally and in person. If your spouse is out of town, it's okay to use the phone.

And use your spouse's name when you give the compliments. For example: "Sandy, you are a beautiful woman." Using the name makes it more personal and, therefore, more positive.

I want each of you to write a list of fourteen compliments for your spouse. I call this the Fabulous Fourteen. Two compliments a day for seven days equals fourteen. That's about the extent of my math ability. These compliments must be truthful and positive. Don't say things like, "Your breath isn't that bad," or "You're not a serial killer," or "At least you helped me have kids."

Your list of compliments can cover a variety of areas: physical attractiveness, character traits, personality, positive and helpful behaviors, and spiritual qualities. Force yourself to think of the positives about your spouse. Cranking out a list of fourteen negatives would be a piece of cake, wouldn't it? However, we are working hard to *eliminate* the negative and bring in the positive.

Keep your Fabulous Fourteen list of compliments in a private place where your spouse will not see it. As you deliver each compliment, check it off the list.

Here are Steve and Sharon's list of compliments. Some of you may remember that one of Sharon's Top Two behaviors is giving Steve one compliment per day. So she will have to give Steve *three* compliments a day during Week 4. Lucky her.

Steve's Fabulous Fourteen

1. You have a wonderful smile.
2. Your eyes are lovely.
3. You are a terrific mom.
4. I love your laugh.
5. You're a great cook.
6. You've really worked to reduce your spending and I appreciate that.
7. Thanks for working so I could finish my education.
8. I admire your honesty; you are a very truthful person.
9. You care about others and do things to help them.
10. You keep our home clean and organized.
11. You're very good at your job.
12. You are beautiful.
13. I love the way you love Jesus and work to grow spiritually.
14. I like your bubbly, expressive personality.

Sharon's Fabulous Fourteen

1. You've got a good sense of humor.
2. You work hard at your job and are a good provider.
3. Thank you for praying with me lately—it means a lot to me.
4. I love your hair—I always have.
5. I like the way you take care of your parents.
6. You are generous and kind.
7. Thanks for loving the kids and spending time with them.
8. You've been patient with my overspending.
9. You take good care of the cars, the home, and the yard.
10. I find you physically attractive.

11. You're having regular quiet times with God, and I like that.
12. Thank you for stepping up to do more chores.
13. Thank you for always being supportive of my time with friends.
14. Thanks for not giving up on us.

Communication Skills

For the last three weeks you've been having at least four twenty-to-thirty-minute Couple Talk Times each week. You've been using my three-step process: a Brief Prayer, a Couple's Devotional, and What's on Your Mind?

Now, in Week 4, I want you to get deeper and closer in your Couple Talk Times. Talking is good. Talking on a deep level and feeling intimately connected is better. Your relationship desperately needs this deeper, more intimate level of communication.

To reach this level, you need to add three communication skills to your Couple Talk Times.

CARRYOVER TOPICS

True conversational intimacy never happens in just one sitting, in one conversation, about a topic. It happens over the course of several conversations over several days. Most couples don't understand this key talking strategy. Like most couples, you and your spouse talk briefly about one topic and then drop it. It never comes up again.

To build real closeness in communication, you need to use Carryover Topics in the What's on Your Mind? step. The idea here is to talk about the same topic two, three, or even four times over the course of a week. Each time you talk about the topic, you get a little deeper.

Let me show you how this works. Let's say Steve and Sharon schedule their four Couple Talk Times for Monday, Tuesday, Thursday, and Saturday. On Monday, they talk about a very painful, stressful situation some good friends are going through. The topic sparks some interest and some strong emotions, and they spend five or ten minutes discussing it. They both recognize that this is a Carryover Topic, a topic that has potential for more intimacy. They agree to think about it and process it over the next day and bring it up again during the What's on Your Mind? segment of their Tuesday Couple Talk Time.

Steve and Sharon discuss their friends' situation again on Tuesday, getting a little deeper this time. Their friends' struggle has triggered memories of similar painful events in their families of origin. In this Tuesday meeting, they each share stories from their childhood years and the emotions they experienced when these events took place. There's some talk about how they feel these past events shaped their lives.

Steve and Sharon are getting deeper in communication, aren't they? Are they done yet? No way! They're on a roll. They continue talking about this Carryover Topic during their Thursday and Saturday Couple Talk Times. They get deeper and feel closer each time they discuss this same topic.

In this process, they are getting to know each other better, getting to know one another's feelings about important things, things that seldom if ever come up.

Whatever the Carryover Topic, talk about it two, three, or four times over the course of Week 4. Between talks, try writing your thoughts and reactions to the topic. In this way, you both will be preparing to go deeper at your next conversation. Jotting down notes about a Carryover Topic is especially helpful for men, because we don't have memories.

PRAYER TOGETHER

You've been praying very briefly in the first step of your Couple Talk Times. Now, in Week 4, I want you to add a five-minute prayer time as a new fourth step. This prayer time will come immediately after the What's on Your Mind? step.

Husband, as the spiritual leader in the marriage relationship, *use a pad and make a list of prayer requests.* Each of you will contribute requests (and concerns). You'll list items that are important to you and to those you love: your marriage, your kids, family members, friends, your church and its leaders, job issues, health concerns, stresses, money problems. . . .

The wife will choose some items to pray for, and the husband will choose some. Then, holding hands, you'll pray one at a time. It will take five minutes or fewer.

Praying out loud can be very difficult, especially if you're not used to doing it. Plus, your marriage is in bad shape and you won't feel like praying with your spouse. I urge you to pray out loud anyway.

By praying, you are inviting God into your relationship and allowing him to change you both. Prayer creates depth. It is an intensely personal activity. It's more intimate than sex in its unique way.

Praying together for five minutes will connect you on a spiritual level. *Spiritual oneness will be the most important factor in your new, healthy marriage.* I'll talk more about spiritual intimacy later in the book, but this prayer time begins the process. (See my book *A Marriage After God's Own Heart* for a thorough description of spiritual intimacy.)

If one of you really feels uncomfortable praying out loud, it's okay for you to pray silently during the first two Couple Talk Times of Week 4. When that partner's prayer ends, he or she simply squeezes the spouse's hand to signal that.

It's important for you silent partners to pray out loud beginning with the third Talk Time. You don't have to pray for long. Just squeezing out a few words is a great achievement. God loves to hear from his children, and he will be pleased. And it will get easier.

Prayer to Conversation

The third communication tool for Week 4 is adding a final step to your Couple Talk Times: Prayer to Conversation.

This step comes immediately after the five-minute Prayer Together step.

When you finish praying, talk about some of the things you just prayed about. These are the concerns of your heart, the important persons and situations you care most deeply about. By following up on your prayer topics, you bridge from prayer to conversation. You will experience, with practice, a deeper level of spiritual and emotional intimacy.

Sandy and I have found that talking about the topics we've just prayed about has greatly enriched our intimacy. When we do the five-minute prayer, we have spiritually bonded and we feel God's blessing. We are already on a deeper level.

When we segue to conversation, we have the topics we will discuss: the things we prayed about. Our conversations about our prayer topics flow more easily and are deeper and more personal. It's as if God is helping us to talk!

If we haven't achieved real depth in the What's on Your Mind? step, we usually get it in the Prayer to Conversation step. Sometimes, we get a deeper connection in both steps!

Because your marriage is where it is now, it will take some time for you to experience true emotional and spiritual intimacy in your Couple Talk Times. Don't get discouraged. You'll get there.

You'll have plenty of opportunities to practice because I want you to keep using these five steps (a Brief Prayer, a Couple's Devotional, What's on Your Mind?, Prayer Together, and Prayer to Conversation) in your Couple Talk Times for the rest of the 90 days.

Homework: Week 4

1. Continue to do the Week 1 pillars: (1) improving your relationship with the Lord, (2) working with your accountability partner, and (3) having your four Couple Talk Times per week.

2. Add one Caring Behavior to your Top Two. Do your Top Three every day during Week 4.
3. Write your Fabulous Fourteen list of compliments and deliver to your spouse—in person, if possible—two compliments a day.
4. Use Carryover Topics as part of the What's on Your Mind? step in your Couple Talk Times. Choose a Carryover Topic in your first Talk Time and continue to talk about it during each of the four Talk Times.
5. Add the two new steps to your Couple Talk Times: Prayer Together and Prayer to Conversation.

6

A Little Bit of Romance Goes a Long Way

Being romantic is difficult for every married couple. At least, it is after the supercharged infatuation stage ends with a thud. Sandy and I have a pretty romantic relationship. We work hard at it. We've found that doing romantic things on a regular basis feeds our feelings of love and passion.

But it's not easy being romantic. Take, for example, our recent viewing of one of the all-time greatest world-class chick movies. I refer to none other than *The Phantom of the Opera*.

Right now, all the men reading this are thinking, "Oh no! You poor, pitiful sucker!" All the women are thinking, "Oh yes! I love that movie! How romantic! I want to see it again—tonight!" Sorry, guys.

Sandy wanted to watch *The Phantom* with me. I like to make her happy, so I said yes. She said it was terribly romantic. Turns out, she had the "terrible" part right.

When Sandy said it was a musical, I should have known what I was in for. I hate musicals. I always have. If I want to hear singing, I'll turn on the radio or put a CD on. Movies are supposed to be filled with snappy dialogue and suspense and a lot of bad guys dying horrible deaths.

Anyway, we settled on our couch to watch *The Phantom of the Opera*. I say settled, because it was unbelievably long. Well over two hours. I thought it would never end. I seriously thought I was going to die before it ended. At one point, I hoped I would die before it ended.

Sandy was entranced. I was nauseated. The heroine, Christine, is a clueless airhead who falls for a monster with half his face covered in a grotesque mask. She allows the Phantom to take her deep into the bowels of his dark, sinister, creepy hideout under the opera house. In such an idyllic scenario, what could possibly go wrong?

Instead of screaming her guts out and running for her life, Christine begins to warm up to the Phantom. He is actually winning her over. Then she tries to peel off his mask. He has a major fit, and it finally dawns on her that this guy has serious anger management issues.

But enough about the insipid plot and awful overacting. It was all the incessant *singing* that drove me nuts. The actors sang just about every line of dialogue in the movie! They would launch into song for lines that didn't need to be set to music: "I have to go to the bathroom," "You're stepping on my foot," "There's a stain on my dress" . . .

Your Week of Romance Is Here

Okay, here's my point: Creating romance is difficult for all married couples. Even for couples who are doing well and who are happy together. For couples who are *not* happy, romance is extremely difficult.

But you must—I repeat, must—pump some romance into your marriage. It will take tremendous effort. It will take everything you have. It will be the exact opposite of what you feel like doing. Do it anyway. Because squeezing even a little bit of romance into your relationship is essential at this point in the 90-Day Change process.

Bring Back the Romance

Week 5 is your week of romance. The good news is, I won't recommend that you watch *The Phantom of the Opera*. The tough news is, I will recommend a variety of romantic actions that will be very challenging to accomplish.

It All Starts with the *Song*

We saw in Chapter 5 how Solomon and Shulamith were the most positive couple who ever lived. Guess what? They were also the most *romantic* couple who ever lived. Solomon and Shulamith were masters at creating romantic situations. They weren't winging it. They knew exactly what actions would lead to deep romantic connections.

In the Song of Solomon, the two lovers are engaged in a variety of romantic behaviors. Frankly, you're not ready yet for everything Solomon and Shulamith did in the romantic arena. But you *are* ready, in Week 5, for two types of romance from Solomon and Shulamith's repertoire: Play and Physical Touch.

In my personal and professional opinion, play and physical touch are *foundational* elements of true romance. They generate a solid introductory base of romance that prepares you for more intimate, personal romantic experiences down the road. Being playful and touching in certain specific ways is the best way to find your way back into romance.

Read the Song

There's one thing you need to do before carrying out the playful and physical touch behaviors. On the first day of Week 5, I want each of you to sit down—separately and in a private, quiet place—and read the Song of Solomon. Read the entire book in one sitting.

Before you read it, pray that God will use the Song to stir your heart and prepare you for the romantic behaviors you'll be doing this week. There are two reasons why God *will* answer this prayer.

One, God's Word as expressed in the Bible is "living and active. Sharper than any double-edged sword, it penetrates even to dividing soul and spirit, joints and marrow; it judges the thoughts and attitudes of the heart" (Heb. 4:12).

Saying that the Bible packs a wallop is a gross understatement. It is, literally, God's Word. When you read it, it is God speaking directly to *you*. It will slice through every obstacle and change your heart. Your life. Your marriage.

Two, the Song of Solomon is unique among the sixty-six books of the Bible. It is the world's most powerful, effective, and beautifully written book on marriage. (*I Don't Want a Divorce* is, of course, a close second.) The Song is the real story of two lovers who knew how to generate and maintain genuine love. Reading their story will touch you and begin to open your heart to your spouse.

When you've finished reading the Song of Solomon, you're ready to start being romantic.

Play, by Watching a Romantic Movie

As soon as possible following your reading of the Song (the same day is ideal), I want the two of you to watch a romantic movie together. Your instructions are to watch the movie in the evening, sitting together on a couch in your home, in low light, and with no children present. Where children are, romance dies. Don't allow a pet in the room with you.

I have three romantic comedies I recommend. My extensive research has shown that these movies do the best job of stirring up playful feelings in couples. And *being playful* is a big part of romance.

Here are the movies: *His Girl Friday*, with Cary Grant and Rosalind Russell, *What's Up Doc?* with Barbra Streisand and Ryan O'Neal, and *While You Were Sleeping*, with Sandra Bullock and Bill Pullman.

These movies are clean, zany, madcap, and very funny romantic adventures. They are guaranteed to make you laugh and imagine being in a playful, romantic relationship with that other person on the couch.

Play, by Going Out on a Date

It may have been a while since you went out on a true date together. Dating is what sweethearts do, and it's time you started getting back into sweetheart mode. My instructions are to go out on a one-, two-, or three-hour "playful" date this week. It could be an evening out or during the day on the weekend.

For this first date, I want the husband to ask the wife out and do the planning for the date. Why does the husband go first? Because the Bible says you are the leader in the marriage relationship (Eph. 5:22–24). Ask her out early in the week: "Honey, would you like to go out with me this Saturday?"

She'll say yes, because I'm ordering her to say yes. No matter how small a sum, you do not invest the money in this book and then *not* follow its instructions.

Husband, plan a date that will bring the two of you together in a playful, creative, and fun way. Don't do the same old, in-a-rut, boring dinner-and-a-movie date. You need to interact in an activity you know she (note, *she*) enjoys: shopping at the mall (I told you this romantic stuff would be difficult), visiting an art or craft fair (no, I'm not trying to punish you), walking on the beach or by a lake or river, picnicking in the park and tossing a Frisbee around, in-line skating, hiking a nature trail, going to a museum, playing golf or tennis . . .

Think back to the things you did when you were courting. Plan a date that will give you plenty of time to talk and have fun together. If you want to make sure you plan a winner of a date, ask her what she'd like to do.

Oh, and one more thing, husband. It's your job to get the babysitter. You'd better have a list of at least three teenage girls (once they get a boyfriend, it's the big kiss-off). If you can get a family member to stay with your kids for free, great. Or maybe you can babysit another couple's kids, and they can return the favor a few days later.

Touch, by Holding Hands

Get ready. Suck it up. "Gird up your loins." Bite the bullet. We are moving into the area of physical touch. Touch is vitally important to every love relationship. Without touch, the best you can ever be is friends. Regular, meaningful touch moves you into the category of lovers. And that's where you're headed.

My Week 5 crash course in physical touch begins with holding hands. It's a simple, basic, and low-key way to introduce touch into your relationship. It's a warm and personal connection. It generates a romantic feeling. (Any touch must be very clearly gentle, tender—always.)

Sandy and I enjoy going to the beach. It's one of our favorite places. Living in Tampa, Florida, allows us to go frequently. We regularly drive to the beach in the evening so we can walk hand in hand, as the sun sets. Romantic? You'd better believe it.

I can always tell the couples who are not married. They are the ones holding hands as they walk down the beach. I can't believe the number of couples who have the nerve to stroll on the beach without holding hands! The sun is setting into the water, there is a beautiful breeze, the sky is alive with color, and scores of couples are not touching at all! Their hands are swinging free!

I make it a habit to walk up to these non-touching couples and say, "Excuse me. I'm a Christian psychologist, and I'm doing a little research here on the beach. Are you married?" They reply, "Yes, we are." I say, "Well, then, why aren't you holding hands in this gorgeous setting? What's the matter with you? You're taking up space that could be used by married couples who want to hold hands and produce a romantic vibe! Get off the beach!"

If you don't want me to track you down and give you the third degree, hold hands this week every chance you get: walking in and out of church, the mall, stores, restaurants, and your home. I also recommend holding hands—at least for a few minutes—when you're sitting in church, in your car, on the couch when you are watching television, and during your Couple Talk Times.

Touch, by Giving Massages

Holding hands is good. (It will always be good.) It's a start. But I want you to get a little more personal and intimate this week in the area of touch. A good, healthy massage feels wonderful and is very romantic. The couples I see in therapy and speak to in my marriage seminars usually have no idea what a good, healthy massage is.

There is nothing quite as disappointing as a half-hearted, lame, two- or three-minute massage. This kind of "I'm doing this, but my heart isn't in it" massage is pathetic. Wimpy. Frankly, it's an insult to the body and person being touched. It's like giving a swallow of water to an individual dying of thirst and then grabbing the canteen away and saying, "That's enough!"

A real massage is at least ten minutes long and involves concentrated effort. If you're the one doing the massaging, put your heart and fingers into it. Ask the massage recipient—frequently—if your massage is pleasing him or her. Encourage him or her to vocally express pleasure and signal that at any time. Be willing to follow the recipient's instructions.

A real massage isn't about relieving a sore back, neck, or shoulders. It isn't about tired, achy feet. It's about expressing romance and love through touch. When spouses ask for a massage, they're asking, "Would you show your love for me by touching me?"

I have a chronically sore neck. It comes from sitting all day working with struggling couples. I love it when Sandy massages my neck. It relieves my pain, but more importantly, I love the feeling of being touched, which is probably a universal feeling. It makes me feel close to Sandy. The massage creates romantic feelings between us.

Here's a little secret: Sometimes, my neck isn't sore at all when I ask Sandy for a massage. I just want her touch and the romantic feeling that comes with it. Is that so wrong? I don't think so.

Your assignment is to give your spouse one ten-minute massage every day during Week 5. That's right. Every day. So to be clear: Each of you will get a daily massage. Don't make your spouse ask for the massage. You do the asking every day: "When do you want your massage today, dear?"

When your spouse gives you a time, you follow up with your second question: "And what part of your beautiful body would you like me to massage?" You probably already know what part, but ask anyway. Everyone has a certain body part he or she enjoys being massaged: scalp, neck, shoulders, back, buttocks, legs, feet.

Don't engage in genital contact when you massage. That will happen down the road when your marriage is reinvigorated with closeness and intimacy in which there is a direct connection between the touch and genuine feelings of love.

Touch, by Kissing and Hugging

You must get your kissing and hugging back. These intimate and sensual physical connections are a vital part of bringing romance back into your marriage. You know how to genuinely and passionately kiss and hug each other. So do it. You used to do it all the time. You're just terribly out of practice.

If you have kissed at all these days, your kisses are miserably poor imitations of the real thing. You're giving incredibly brief "pecks." You're delivering "air kisses." Or, worst of all, you're actually doing "cheek kisses." Stop it! Stop kissing this way! It's embarrassing, and it's draining the life out of what's left of your marriage.

Hugging—real, full-body, sensual hugging—is also a dim memory. If you hug at all, you hug like a couple of sticks: both stiff as boards. Or you do the inverted V hug: stand at a distance and gingerly lean forward and barely touch shoulders. Or the miserable side hug: sneak up to the spouse's side, put an arm carefully around the shoulders, and pull gently. Stop it! Stop hugging this way! It's okay to hug a long-lost aunt this way. But not your spouse.

In Week 5, we're going to roll back the clock and go back to revive the kind of kissing and hugging you did when you were in love. Are you ready for this? You say you're not? Tough. You need to do it anyway.

Every day this week, I want you to kiss and hug each other twice. The kiss and hug will be at the same time. I'd prefer one hug-and-kiss "event" in the morning and one in the evening. For example, a hug and a kiss before you leave for work and another hug and kiss when you see each other after the workday.

Of course, your schedules may prevent you from following this once-in-the-morning and once-in-the-evening plan. No problem. You can kiss and hug at the end of the workday and then again just before bed. As long as you do two hug-and-kiss events a day, no matter how much time comes between them, you've done your jobs.

Here's how I want you to hug and kiss. The hug comes first. Do a total body contact, face-to-face, wraparound hug. Your bodies are pressed together. Arms wrapped around each other. Firm pressure. Hold the clinch between five and ten seconds; longer is also good.

As you release from the hug, stay close to each other as you prepare for the kiss. Gently holding each other's shoulders or each other's faces, plant a five-second smoocher directly on the lips. Almost always, you'll find his or her lips directly beneath that person's nose. A bit of moisture wouldn't hurt, but I'm not expecting too much yet.

Your first few hugs and kisses won't be impressive. They will be awkward and stilted. Keep on hugging and kissing twice a day, and you'll start to loosen up and get into it. It's like muscle memory. The ability to romantically hug and kiss will come back, along with wonderful feelings of love and passion.

I want you to continue these romantic behaviors in the areas of play and physical touch—with the exception of romantic movies—for the remainder of the 90 days.

In Weeks 4 and 5, you have established some much needed positive flow in your marriage. It's very important to *maintain* this flow, because there's difficult work coming up in the 90-day program. Your new positivity and romanticity (I know it's not a real word, but you see what I mean) will help you get through these next few weeks.

Homework: Week 5

1. Continue to improve your personal relationship with God, stay in contact with your accountability partner, and have your four Couple Talk Times.
2. Read, on your own, in one sitting, the entire book of the Song of Solomon. Before reading the Song, pray that God will use his Word to touch your heart and prepare you to carry out the Week 5 romantic behaviors.
3. As soon as possible after reading the Song of Solomon, watch together one of the romantic movies I suggested.
4. With the husband doing the planning and the asking, go out on a playful date.
5. Hold hands at every opportunity.
6. Give each other ten-minute, heartfelt massages once a day.
7. Hug and kiss each other—in the way I described—twice each day.

7

Conflict-Resolving Skills That Work

Put a married couple together in the same living space, and you will have conflict. A lot of conflict. Disagreements involving anger and hurt feelings don't happen just in the stages of marital breakdown, but throughout the *entire life span* of the marriage. Conflicts will occur with amazing frequency as long as you both shall live.

You can't change your marriage until you and your mate learn the skill of conflict resolution.

The question is not, do you have conflict? If you're both alive, you have conflict. The question is not, can you avoid conflict? Avoiding it is impossible. The question is, how do you handle your conflict?

You and your spouse have two choices: You can handle conflict poorly or well. Handling conflict poorly will inevitably lead to a dead relationship. It won't die immediately, but it will die over time, a slow, agonizing death. Every time you fail to resolve a conflict, you're a little further apart. Eventually, you are miles apart, and no love is left.

Handling your conflict well will lead to an intimate relationship. Your disagreements create sparks and relational intensity, which, if handled correctly, produce deep emotional connection. Every time you successfully work through a conflict, the two of you will be a little closer. Each resolved conflict brings a greater knowledge of one another, which results in a greater love for one another.

Resolved conflicts are one of the main avenues to passion.

Learn How to Fight

It's easy for me to tell you to handle your conflict well. *But to actually do it, you must know how.* Most husbands and wives have no idea how to resolve conflict successfully. They know how *not* to do it, and their dysfunctional pattern is killing their marriages.

Chances are very good that you resolve conflict in the same ineffective way your parents did. No one has ever taught you a step-by-step formula for successful conflict resolution. I'm going to do that right now. My formula for fair fighting isn't complicated. It's not rocket science. It's simple. But when you learn it through practice, it will work.

The Right Time and Place

When conflict first hits, and words expressing anger are just starting to come out of your mouth, you must call an immediate cease-fire, and each of you must go to a neutral corner. You say, "But we haven't even begun to talk about it yet!" I reply, "Exactly. When anger initially hits, no one is ready to talk about it."

Many couples make the mistake of trying to talk about a conflict too quickly. Sandy and I made this mistake for years until we figured out it was a disaster and that it just made our conflicts worse.

When a conflict surfaces, you are not ready to deal with it yet. Tempers are high. The level of emotional intensity is at its peak. You're running on adrenaline. You're fueled by the "flight or fight" syndrome. You're not thinking clearly, and your mouth will go into overdrive. Both of you will say things you don't mean, and damage will be done. And, of course, the conflict has no chance of being resolved.

"The tongue is a small part of the body, and yet it boasts of great things. See how great a forest is set aflame by such a small fire! And the tongue is a fire, the very world of iniquity" (James 3:5–6 NASB). Sound familiar? How many times have you acted out this verse in a conflict? Yeah. Me too. This is not what you want as your life verse.

It's natural to want to launch immediately into a conflict and go back and forth over the issue. When you've been stung, your mouth is triggered and you want to sting back to "clarify the issue," state your case, defend yourself—right now. There is usually one partner who wants to talk it out right away and get it resolved. No! Don't do it. It's a bad idea. Here's the wisdom of Solomon: "The beginning of strife is like letting out water, so abandon the quarrel before it breaks out" (Prov. 17:14 NASB).

Here's what I want you to do when a conflict begins. Tell your partner, "I'm angry, we have a problem to deal with, and I'll let you know when I'm ready to discuss it." Then skedaddle away from your partner and the scene of the potential crime. You need to get space as soon as possible. The less talking in this first phase of conflict resolution the better. Again in Proverbs we read, "There is one who speaks rashly like the thrusts of a sword" (12:18 NASB). Don't even attempt to schedule the time and place for the discussion. That's too much talking, and there's a huge risk of saying something you'll regret.

Each of you needs to go to a private place to cool down and pray for God's help to deal with the conflict. Even a few minutes will help you calm down from your peak of emotional intensity. You may still be angry and hurt, but not furious and in full battle mode.

When you have simmered down and feel prepared to begin the discussion of the conflict, go to your partner (or call on the telephone) and say, "I'm ready to talk now. Let me know when you are ready." When your spouse indicates readiness, schedule the time and place for the conflict discussion.

The time ought to be as soon as possible, once you are both ready. Ephesians 4:26–27 states, "Be angry and yet do not sin; do not let the sun go down on your anger, and do not give the devil an opportunity" (NASB). You probably won't get all the way through the conflict on the first day, but God clearly wants your anger to be expressed and released in a harmless, non-threatening way—"speaking the truth in love" (Eph. 4:15)—before the end of the first day.

The place should be a location in your home that is private, quiet, and neutral. The children should not overhear your discussion. This doesn't mean that you hide from them the truth that Mom and Dad have disagreements and disputes, but that you resolve them. By neutral, I mean not warm and cozy and intimate. Don't use your bedroom or the special place you use for your Couple Talk Times. I usually recommend the kitchen or dining room table. When you choose a conflict place, agree that this will be the location you will use to discuss most of your conflicts. It helps to limit and contain your conflict resolutions to one spot. It provides structure and control.

Obviously, if one of you is out of town, you won't be able to use this location, and you will have to use the phone for the first part of the conflict discussion.

One at a Time

When you are seated in your conflict location, sufficiently cooled down and individually "prayed up," pray out loud for God's help to work through the conflict. I prefer that both spouses pray briefly, just a sentence or two; if only one will pray, I strongly recommend it be the husband. Spiritual leadership. Enough said.

After a short prayer, one spouse will go first and share his or her feelings, thoughts, and point of view about the disagreement. This spouse is the *Speaker*, which makes the other spouse the *Listener*. For this stage and the next stage of the conflict resolution process, you will stay rigidly attached to these Speaker-Listener roles. Communication will be one at a time. There must be one Speaker and one Listener at all times, with no interchange or interruptions. If both spouses speak, there is no understanding occurring and therefore no movement toward resolution. If both spouses speak, the two tongues take over, and the result is chaos and raised voices and nasty comments and a big, fat, ugly mess.

The Speaker, in ten minutes or fewer, says what he or she needs to say about the issue. The Speaker shares his or her opinion, feelings, and position. The Listener may disagree, but what the Speaker says can't be wrong; it is the Speaker's truth. To oppose it is saying, "You can't feel that way! I deny you the right to feel that way or have your beliefs about it."

The Listener's job is to say nothing original, but rather to help the Speaker feel understood. The Listener achieves this understanding and clearly shows this understanding to his or her spouse by being an *active listener*, which means reflecting back what the Speaker is saying and the feelings being expressed. To be true to what the Speaker has said, the Listener should use the Speaker's words rather than his or her own.

In other words, the Listener stuffs his or her own feelings and point of view for the moment and focuses on the Speaker's message and making sure the Speaker feels understood.

The Listener says things like: "You're saying that my comment about your sister made you feel angry and hurt." "You wonder if I've ever liked your sister." "You're deeply offended, because you love your sister and feel close to her." "It's important to you that I respect your family and at least get along with your sister." "Is that right?"

You don't move on until the Speaker confirms that the Listener understands. Although the Speaker's opening statement has a ten-minute limit (it is often a good idea to set a timer), it may take longer to achieve understanding. Take the time needed to clarify the Speaker's message, because this first link of understanding is critical. Without a connection here, resolution has no chance of happening.

Keep in mind that I'm talking about *understanding*, not agreement. You're going to disagree, that's why they call it a conflict. Besides, you're a man and a woman. You disagree on a lot of things anyway. There will always be two points of view and two sets of feelings in every conflict. *You are both right*. What we are doing is working for both of you to get the understanding of your respective truths.

When understanding has been reached because the Speaker at the time says so, it's time for a break. Let the achieved understanding rest for a while so that it truly takes hold. If the Listener takes his or her turn too soon, cranks up right away, and begins sharing his or her truth, the delicate, newborn understanding of the Speaker's truth can be wiped out.

So leave your seats for a bit—ten minutes at a minimum. It might be half an hour, one hour, or even two hours. I prefer a short time if it's possible. Remember, you are dealing essentially with one issue, not all the complaints or bad feelings of the past ten years. If the Listener is really struggling with anger and other intense emotions, or wrestling with the Speaker's message, it will take longer to settle before the Listener takes his or her turn as Speaker.

After the break, return to your seats and reverse roles. The Listener is now the Speaker, and vice versa. The new Speaker will share his or her feelings, opinions, and point of view about the same issue introduced by the Speaker. The new Speaker will now present a second truth and set of feelings, which are as equally valid as the first Speaker's. It is the new Listener's job to reflect what he or she hears and to work toward understanding. Follow the same process as with the first Speaker, allowing the new Speaker up to ten minutes to state his or her case.

The truth expressed by the second Speaker may be totally different from what the first Speaker said. It may represent a totally different point of view and set of emotions. No one is lying. As you would expect, a different person of a different gender is most likely going to express a different truth.

Take the time to build this second bridge of understanding. Don't move on until the new Speaker feels understood and says so. You don't have to agree, which is a good thing because you won't. You can't! Regardless of the issue, you will see it and feel it in your way. Same for your partner. But you can and must work to understand and fully validate your partner's feelings and point of view.

Processing

When the two truths have been expressed, and both spouses feel understood, it's time for another break. Let the two understandings resonate and settle in for a while. The good news is that, at this point, you are three-quarters of the way to resolution. The bad news is that you're not done yet, and it's easy to mess it up unless you follow the guidelines.

Your break may last just ten minutes, or it may last until the next day. If you're getting the impression that conflict requires time to resolve, you're right. Slow and steady is the way to successful resolution. You'll need this break to think about what has already happened and mull it over in your heart and mind. The anger is out and largely released, so you've obeyed Ephesians 4:26–27. But you need to let your brains rest and process the issues that have been discussed.

When you're ready to continue the conflict discussion, let your partner know. When your partner signals readiness, schedule a time to resume talking in your conflict-resolution place.

When you get back to it, you will still take turns as Speaker and Listener. I call this the Processing stage because you will review the topics and emotions already shared in an attempt to solidify understanding and emotional connection. You will work for clarification. You will do more venting of emotions, if necessary, but *not ever* to hurt or punish your mate. You will seek reassurance that your spouse really does understand you.

The wife, because she is a woman, especially needs this Processing stage. A woman typically has to go over an issue several times before she can release it. She processes more than a man will and does it out loud more than he does. That's okay. She needs to do it, so her husband should let her do it without any hesitancy or impatience on his part. She needs to fully express herself and be confident that her ideas and feelings are fully understood.

If, at the end of the Processing stage, you have talked out your truths until you both feel understood and reconnected, and if there is no decision to be made, you're done! But if your conflict requires a decision of some kind, you will move on to the Let's Make a Deal stage.

"Let's Make a Deal"

Before you start the Let's Make a Deal stage, guess what you're going to do? That's right—take another break. This break should be from a few minutes to half a day or more. When both partners are ready to resume, agree on a time and return one more time to your conflict-resolution location.

If you must decide on some course of action or some behavior—a financial move, a parenting strategy, a schedule change, or something you want your partner to do or not to do—you will need to work together to make a deal. With most of the anger gone and a substantial amount of understanding achieved, you will be in good shape to negotiate and reach an agreement. It is usually okay to go back and forth in this stage without staying in the Speaker-Listener roles. But if things begin to get too intense, go right back to these roles.

Pray again as you enter this decision stage. God will help you hammer out a deal. Agree on specific behaviors that can be measured. Avoid vague decisions like, "Let's see if we can do better." What does such a statement mean? Nobody knows.

Here's an example of a good, tight, specific deal:

Wife: I'd be happy if you would at least call me before 5:00 p.m. every workday and tell me when you expect to get home. Even if you're going to be late, it will help me to know in advance.

Husband: Okay. I'll call you every day before 5:00 p.m. and let you know when I expect to get home.

Be willing to compromise. You won't get your way every time. Sometimes you'll get your way, and sometimes your spouse will get his or hers. Sometimes you'll meet in the middle with a deal that includes ideas from both of you.

Every deal is on a trial basis. If it doesn't work, call a meeting and go back to the table and renegotiate. Don't make a deal you don't like. Stay at this renegotiation until you reach a decision you both can live with.

Take It Slowly

It will take a minimum of two days to work through the vast majority of your conflicts. Do not expect to get through in one sitting. Unless it's an extremely minor conflict, it simply can't be done. You can get your anger out by the end of the first day, but the whole process takes time. It will take two, three, or even four days to successfully resolve a conflict. More intense, nastier conflicts could easily take a week or more.

It's important to nurture your relationship in other areas as you work through a conflict. Talk about other subjects in your regular Couple Talk Times. Continue to go out on playful dates, hold hands, give each other massages, and hug and kiss. A conflict doesn't need to grind your relationship and the positives you're building to a halt, especially after the initial anger is released and dissipates. You can develop the skill of maintaining a positive flow as a couple while the conflict-resolution process is running its course.

Stop and Start

When a conflict conversation gets off track, even slightly, shut it down immediately. Don't try to save it by trying to get back to a good place. You can't do that. No couple can. That conversation is over. Take a time-out right away, and leave your conflict location. Either spouse can call for a stop, and it must be honored. It might be just five minutes. When you're ready to resume, tell your partner and ask him or her to find you when ready. Then sit down again and start back up where you left off.

If the husband raises his voice, stop, take a break, and start again. If the wife talks way beyond her ten-minute limit, and the husband is getting frustrated and overwhelmed, stop, take a break, and restart. If the wife shuts down and clams up, stop, take a break, and restart. If the husband won't honor a break and follows his wife down the hall talking, stop, take a break, and restart. Any violation of the Speaker-Listener rules should also trigger a stop, break, restart.

No matter what happens to disturb the operation of the conflict-resolution formula, you need to stop and restart. As you learn how to follow these steps, you'll stop and start frequently. That's acceptable. It's healthy and normal and a lot better than chewing on each other and going back to your old way of fighting.

Practice, Practice, Practice

You've heard the phrase "Practice makes perfect." This is an overstatement. There's no such thing as perfect, especially in marriage. But practice does make better. A lot better.

It's time to practice your new conflict-resolving knowledge. You now know the steps. To make the steps into a skill, you need to practice. And practice. And practice.

Since you'll be having conflict the rest of your marriage, you'd better get used to the process of resolving it effectively.

Here in Week 6, pick two recent conflicts you've faced, and practice working through them one at a time. Choose two conflicts that are small—more irritating than angering. Do not choose conflicts that involve intense anger. It's far easier to learn these conflict-resolving skills on minor irritations.

After your practice in Week 6, you'll have a better handle on how to talk through a conflict. To further solidify your skills, continue during Weeks 7 and 8 to use my formula on small conflicts that arise.

Again, *do not attempt* to tackle your big, nasty, or long-standing unresolved conflicts yet. I know you are keenly aware of the huge disagreements you've never been able to resolve and the deep, smoldering resentments and hurts you're harboring against each other. Now is *not* the time to face them.

We'll be dealing directly with these "conflict biggies" a bit down the road, in Weeks 9 and 10.

Homework: Week 6

1. Continue to work on improving your relationship with the Lord, stay in contact with your accountability partner, have your four Couple Talk Times per week, go out on one playful date, hold hands, give once-a-day massages, and hug and kiss twice a day.

2. How much conflict do you and your spouse experience? How many conflicts do you usually have in a week? A month?

3. What do you typically fight about? What are the top three or four issues—the ones you fight about over and over?

4. How do you fight? What pattern do you follow when there's a conflict? What does the husband do? What does the wife do? How does not resolving conflicts negatively affect your marriage?

5. Tell your spouse who taught you to deal with conflict. How did your mom and dad express anger? How did your parents fight?

6. Pick two recent conflicts, small and not too intense, and practice working through them using the fair fighting formula that I've described in this chapter (Speaker-Listener, etc.).

7. During Weeks 7 and 8, continue to use the conflict steps on small issues that arise.

8

Heal from Your Past Pain

There are many who strongly believe that the past has nothing to do with the problems in a struggling marriage. I strongly believe just the opposite. The past has a great, ongoing impact on a struggling marriage. In fact, if you fail to address the past, you will have zero chance to heal and rebuild your marriage.

Every person—that's right, every person—has some unresolved issues connected to past relationships. These issues always—that's right, always—transfer to a marriage partner and cause all manner of intimacy-killing mayhem.

A Case in Point

I saw a couple recently whose marriage was on the rocks. They had a nasty, destructive communication pattern that had ruined their relationship. When they discussed an issue, especially an issue over which they disagreed, he was rigidly logical and she was intensely emotional.

He remained in his logical mode and calmly and rationally refuted her arguments. She became increasingly frustrated and felt misunderstood and mistreated. She escalated in emotional intensity and raised her voice. He accused her of overreacting and left the room. She ended up feeling rejected, angry, and deeply hurt.

I showed them that their dysfunctional communication pattern had its roots in their pasts. Her mom spent years getting emotionally intense with her dad in a fruitless quest to get him to listen to her and emotionally connect with her. Her dad used logic to thwart these attempts and refused to open up emotionally. He often left these conversations when her mom got too emotional and loud.

My female client desperately wanted and needed to be emotionally close to her dad. She tried again and again to draw him into conversations, but he stayed in logical mode and refused to listen to her.

Her husband's parents had a cold, emotionless marriage. His dad used logic and intellect to handle all issues in the marriage and the home. His dad did not allow anyone in the family to express any deep, personal emotions. His mom was a weak, passive person who chose to follow his dad's rules. She stuffed her emotions and made no attempts to emotionally connect with her husband. This man was not close to either of his parents.

Her parents taught her to be emotionally intense in a never-ending effort to connect with a man. Since she never succeeded with her dad, her desire to be close to a man grew into a deep need. His parents taught him to avoid all emotion and use logic to handle all relationship issues. He became a master at avoiding any emotional connection with others. Deep down, he needed this closeness with his wife. But he automatically used logic to sidestep it.

Once they realized the power of their pasts and worked—together—to heal from their pasts, they were able to break their old communication pattern and learn a brand-new one. One that worked.

I Transfer, You Transfer, We All Transfer

The transfer problem is a combination of learned behavior and unresolved emotional pain. And it all starts in the home where you grew up.

Your parents' marriage has tremendous influence on the kind of marriage you will develop. You learn how marriage operates from their marriage. All their weaknesses, mistakes, and dysfunctional patterns become your weaknesses, mistakes, and dysfunctional patterns.

In the marriage case I just described, my clients learned what they were doing from their parents. They were simply repeating a communication pattern they learned as children. They couldn't do anything else, because they didn't know anything else!

Your relationship with each parent teaches you how to act in your marriage. Your relationship with your same-sex parent will determine your behavior as a spouse. Your relationship with your opposite-sex parent will determine how you interact with your spouse. Plus, any emotional pain you experienced with a parent remains inside and transfers to your spouse.

My female client above learned from her mom how to be emotionally intense with a man. Her failed efforts to connect with him had caused her deep hurt and disappointment. She carried this learned response into her marriage.

She chose an emotionally unavailable man with whom she could *re-create* the same dysfunctional pattern she had experienced with her dad. She spent years trying to get her husband to open up to her and be close to her. She desperately hoped, deep down, that if she could connect with her husband, her issues with her dad would be healed.

Because of her unresolved father pain, she was way too aggressive in her approach to her husband. Her intensity doomed her efforts.

When her husband repeatedly rebuffed her intense attempts to emotionally engage, she became very angry, hurt, and resentful. Her "dad pain" transferred and fused to her "husband pain" and created a massive ball of resentment inside her. She was angry and bitter at her husband for his behavior *and* at her dad for his behavior.

Her dad pain made her unable to reach out to her husband in a reasonable way. Her dad pain also made her unable to forgive her husband for his rejection of her.

Some of you are thinking, "But both my parents were great, and they had a very good marriage. Doesn't this mean I can avoid all this negative transfer?" No, I'm afraid not. A healthy home is obviously a real advantage. You did learn many positive, effective relationship behaviors, and you probably don't have a large amount of emotional baggage.

However, no parents are perfect. No one gets out of their home unscathed. Your parents each had weaknesses—in their personal lives, in their marriage, and in their parenting. These weaknesses impacted you and have transferred to your spouse.

As you can see, there is a lot of transfer from your parents to your spouse. But hold on. Your parents are only part of the transfer problem. There is also a lot of transfer from other relationships. Every significant relationship prior to the one with your spouse produces a package of learned behaviors and unresolved emotional pain. And all of it transfers to your spouse.

I'm talking about stepparents. Serious dating relationships. Ex-spouses. Also, anyone who caused you harm through physical, psychological, or sexual abuse.

The bad news is, all your old, learned behaviors and unresolved emotional pain transfer directly to your spouse. Your past both creates and energizes your current conflicts with your spouse.

Your spouse becomes the *personification* of all your past issues with others. As a result, two things happen. One, you will be unable to stop re-creating your unhealthy, ineffective relationship pattern. Two, you will be unable to forgive your spouse for his or her hurtful behavior.

All right. Enough bad news. The good news is, you can change your old, learned behavior and heal from unresolved emotional pain. You can eliminate the transfer from the past so that you have to address only the issues between the two of you. You really can start fresh in your marriage.

You Gotta Go Back before You Go Forward

Many marriage counselors, Christian and secular, ignore the past or touch on it only superficially. They immediately focus on a couple's current conflicts and work to build a new marriage. This present-centered therapeutic approach may produce a brief spurt of improvement, but ultimately it will fail.

How can I be so sure? Because early in my career I skipped over the past and worked only on a couple's current problems. It didn't work! I've realized that every couple's current problems were being fueled by the unresolved issues in their pasts. No new, healthy patterns could be established until the old, destructive patterns from the past were dismantled.

When I present my plan to deal with the past, couples often tell me, "But we don't want to live in the past! The past is over, and we want to move on."

I reply, "You are living in the past every day! The past has a hold on you and you can't move on. You can't build a great marriage by living in the past *and* the present. When we clean out the past, *then* we can deal with the present."

After these two weeks of working on your past, you'll still have your nasty, damaging marital patterns. But now you can defeat them. Their power source has been exposed and cut off. And you are closer as a couple because you did the work together.

The Benefits of Stopping the Transfer

When you have worked through the past and stopped the transfer to your spouse, you'll be one step closer to a new marriage. There are seven benefits of doing this work on your past:

1. You will heal as a person. One of the wonderful things about marriage is that it can help us heal from past hurts. God allows the transfer because he wants you both to heal from what happened in your relationships before you got married. When you are a healthier person, you'll be a healthier marriage partner.

2. You will be opened up emotionally. Working on your past pain breaks down barriers to intimacy that have been in place for years. You will learn how to identify emotions and express them. Your past wounds have prevented you from becoming emotionally, spiritually, and physically intimate with your spouse. Your past made you unwilling to risk getting hurt again. Now you can take the risk.

3. You will understand clearly why your marriage is struggling. This step helps you explain why you both act the way you do. The same old mistakes, weaknesses, and reactions now make sense. You see now the "why" of your mistakes, weaknesses, and reactions. You'll feel a softening toward your spouse. It's not that you have terrible problems and just can't get along. It's because of the transfer!

4. You will eliminate the transfer of the past to your spouse. Facing your past is the only way to kill the transfer. With the power of the past broken, you can now dismantle your unhealthy marital patterns and develop new ones.

5. You and your spouse will be closer. By working together on each other's pasts, you will become a better team.

108

Healing together will forge a more intimate bond. You will build empathy by feeling your spouse's past pain. You will comfort and support each other through some painful memories. You'll learn how to communicate more deeply and effectively. Because you have talked about very personal, difficult topics, you'll be able to talk about anything.

6. You will understand the needs of your spouse. You'll see what important needs your spouse didn't get met in past relationships. You'll see that your spouse has those same needs in your marriage.

7. You will be able to forgive your spouse. Now that you have forgiven the people in your past for harming you, those resentments are no longer attached to your spouse. You can now work through your resentments against your spouse, truly forgive, and move on without any lingering bitterness.

I've told you how important it is to deal with your pasts. I've shown you the benefits of going through the process. Now I'm going to tell you exactly how to do it.

The Past Pain Transfer Letters

In Week 7, I want you to write a letter to those people in your past with whom you have had a significant personal relationship: mom, dad, stepparent, grandparent, ex-spouse, ex-dating partner. . . . Mom and Dad (or those caretakers who had a major role in raising you) always make the list because of their powerful influence on your life. People you dated for long periods of time and ex-spouses also make the list because they shaped your behavior in opposite-sex, romantic relationships.

Anyone makes the list who has had a dramatic, lasting impact on your life and how you operate in opposite-sex relationships. A person who abused you makes the list. A person who caused you terrible hurt and pain makes the list.

Most of my clients write three or four letters: mom, dad, an ex-spouse or two, and maybe an old boyfriend or girlfriend. Each letter is typically two to three pages long, but it can certainly be longer if the person being written to caused a lot of emotional pain.

These will be real letters, with sentences and paragraphs. No lists or bullet points. A full-fledged letter is more likely to reveal the truth about these important relationships, the pain you experienced in them, and how they continue to impact your marriage today.

These letters are *not to be mailed.* I want you to write them as if you were going to mail them, but their content will be shared only with your spouse. Each letter will contain two parts: A and B. Part A, the first part, covers the pain you experienced with the person and what you were taught about relationships. Part B describes the specific transfer from this previous relationship to your spouse.

Part A: The Pain and the Learned Behaviors

As you sit down to write, pray that God will give you what you need to put on paper. He knows what you need to express in order to heal and stop the transfer.

The first section of each letter, part A, is devoted to the honest expression of the pain the person caused you and the dysfunctional principles you were taught about relationships. Feel free to mention positives, but don't spend much time on them. It's the negatives that must be exposed. It's the negatives in these past relationships that are causing real problems in your marriage.

Describe the person's personality. What the relationship was like. The person's weaknesses and mistakes. What the person did to hurt you. Select a few painful memories and write what happened and the emotions you experienced. If you made mistakes, mention them, also.

You may be surprised, as many of my clients have been, at the amount and the intensity of pain these letters will bring to the surface. Memories from years ago can still carry a deep level of emotional power. Your emotional response—as you write your letter and, later, as you read your letter—is a good indicator of how deeply you were hurt and where you are in the process of resolving these issues. Let your emotions flow freely. Healing comes through facing painful events and fully expressing your emotions connected to those events.

As you write about what happened and your emotional reaction, include what you believe the person taught you about relationships. What incorrect, ineffective learned behaviors developed out of your painful interactions with this person? "You taught me to always stuff my emotions and pretend everything was okay." "You taught me that the way to handle anger is to raise your voice and rant and rave." "I learned from you that I have to perform if I want to be accepted and loved." "Dad, you taught me that men will always disappoint me, so it's not worth trying to trust them or let them get close."

At the end of part A, write words of forgiveness. You've taken the critical step toward forgiveness by honestly expressing what the person did to hurt you, your emotions when it happened and now because of the harmful treatment, and the impact on you and your relationships. Now it's time to let your resentment and bitterness go, and to forgive. Choosing to forgive someone is a huge step toward eliminating transfer from that person to your spouse.

Part B: The Transfer to Your Marriage

In the second part of each letter, part B, you describe how your pain and learned behaviors with this person are transferring to your spouse. Be as specific as possible. Your work in part A will help illuminate these points of transfer.

"My mom was the queen of denial, and that's why I keep my real emotions hidden from you and fake like everything's fine." "Just as I learned to do with my dad, I rant and rave at you when I'm angry." "The only way to please my ex and get at least some acceptance and love was to kill myself doing all the chores and housework. So that's why I'm doing the same thing in our relationship." "Because my dad disappointed me so many times, I built a wall around me that you can't break through."

I can't overstate the power of seeing clearly how you are repeating in your marriage destructive patterns from past relationships. When you clean out your emotional pain connected to these individuals in the past and identify the transfer, you can finally stop making the same old mistakes with your spouse.

These letters do not have to be long and filled with a mountain of details. Just hit the main points with honesty and openness, and that will get the job done: what happened in the past relationship, how you were affected, your emotions, what you learned about relationships, words of forgiveness, and the specific points of present transfer.

Read Your Letters

I want you to finish your letters in five to six days. It would be ideal for you to be done by Friday, the sixth day of Week 7. This is an intense and difficult assignment, so you'll need to carve out at least three to four hours total to write. It's also best not to do them all in one sitting. That would take too much time and be very emotionally demanding. Chip away at the letters, writing for a half hour at a sitting. Many of my clients write part A, take a break for several hours or a day to process and pray, and then return to complete part B.

Sit down on a Friday evening and begin to read your letters out loud to each other. I recommend you schedule three separate reading times: one on Friday, one on Saturday, and one on Sunday. You'll each read one letter per reading time. Each session will probably last thirty to forty-five minutes. If you have each written three letters (mom, dad, ex-spouse, for example), this schedule will get you through all the reading by Sunday.

You may adjust this time frame if needed. If you finish your letters before Friday, you can start your reading sessions early. If it takes you longer than anticipated to finish writing, you can delay your reading sessions. If you have more than three letters, you'll need more sessions to read them. I would like you to be done with all the reading by Sunday evening, because that will keep you on schedule for the Week 8 Homework.

Here's how a reading session works. You sit down in a private, quiet place in your home. It could be the place you use for your Couple Talk Times. No kids present, of course, and no one within hearing distance. No pets. No distractions. No phone. No interruptions. Pray briefly, out loud, that God will use these letters to help you eliminate toxic transfer in your marriage.

I recommend that you read the letters you have written to your parents first. All your pain and issues in relationships began with them. Also, it works best if the two letters you read per session are letters you both have written to the same person. For example, you could follow this format:

First session: Both read your "mom" letters.

Second session: Both read your "dad" letters.

Third session: Both read your "ex" letters.

The husband reads his letter first in each session. He reads his entire letter while his wife listens attentively and in silence, trying only to comprehend what her husband is saying. These are his experiences and feelings only. When he is done, the wife makes comments that are positive, supportive, and encouraging. Briefly, in five minutes or less, she thanks him for writing the letter and tells him she's going to work to understand what he went through in this past relationship. She may comment on painful memories he related that she wasn't aware of and may mention some transfer points he described that she found especially interesting.

After making her positive and empathetic responses, the wife reads her letter. The process is now reversed, with the husband listening, in silence, concentrating on understanding what she is saying. He then makes his positive and empathetic responses.

You'll follow this same procedure until all the letters are read and the encouraging, understanding words are spoken by the listening spouse. Again, your goal is to be done with your reading sessions by Sunday evening, the end of Week 7.

Week **8**

The Follow-Up Talks

In Week 8, your assignment is to have four Follow-Up Talks about your Past Pain Transfer Letters. Immediately after all the letters are read, give your spouse your letters. Each of you reads your spouse's letters several times during this week in a sincere effort to understand his or her past pain and transfer issues. As you read and reread your spouse's letters, pick out painful memories and learned negative behaviors you want to discuss further. Jot down comments and questions that occur to you as you read and reread the letters.

Take fifteen to twenty minutes at your regularly scheduled Couple Talk Times to have these Follow-Up Talks. Pray briefly before each Follow-Up Talk that God will bless your efforts to recognize and eliminate transfer from past relationships.

It's in these Follow-Up Talks that the support, the understanding, the acceptance, and the empathy truly get reinforced. You'll be talking on a very personal level, and you will create intimate connections. You will heal together and wipe out negative transfer to your marriage.

One final, important point. If you have serious, traumatic past pain—physical, psychological, or sexual abuse, rape, an abortion—you'll need more than two weeks to heal and eliminate the transfer to your spouse. Please, take the time necessary to work through your pain. It may take three to six months or longer. Take the time.

Find a Christian therapist and, with your spouse as your central supporter, face your traumatic pain and heal from it. Typically, you'll do a combination of individual and couple therapy. Once you have healed sufficiently, you and your spouse can return to Weeks 7 and 8 of the Change Your Marriage program and continue the steps.

I've covered what you need to do in Weeks 7 and 8. Now, to make sure you know what to do, let's take a look at these two weeks in the life of one married couple. Your homework is found at the end of Chapter 9.

9

The Pain Is Gone
and We're Moving On

One Couple's Journey
through Weeks 7 and 8

Steve and Sharon have completed Weeks 1 through 6 in my Change Your Marriage program. Weeks 4 and 5 injected some desperately needed positive, romantic flow into their relationship. They tell me they've been practicing new conflict-resolving skills they learned in Week 6.

I go over their Weeks 7 and 8 assignments: The Past Pain Transfer Letters and the Follow-Up Talks.

I tell them: "We're not blaming these people in your pasts for your mistakes in the marriage. Your mistakes are 100 percent your fault. But these Letters and Follow-Up Talks will accomplish three very important goals. One, they'll explain why you act the way you do in your marriage. Two, they'll break the power of the past and eliminate the transfer to your spouse. Three, they'll help you stop making the same old mistakes and start building new, healthy patterns in your marriage."

Here are their letters:

Steve's Letter to His Dad

Dear Dad,

Overall, you were a good father. You worked hard and I never lacked for anything. You came to my games and helped teach me how to play football, baseball, and basketball. But, Dad, you made some big mistakes that have ended up really hurting me.

You were not the spiritual leader in our home. Mom was, because you wouldn't do it. You attended church with us and prayed before meals, but that was about it. You taught me that leading spiritually wasn't important. At the time, I didn't think it was a big deal. Now I know it is, because Sharon needs me to lead her and the kids spiritually.

Dad, I'm angry at you because you blew it in this area. It was your job to show me spiritual leadership and to teach me how to do it.

Dad, I'm also angry and hurt and disappointed because you rarely, if ever, shared your emotions. We did things together, but you didn't talk to me on a personal level. We weren't close. I saw you—many times—avoid Mom's attempts to talk with you. You taught me that a real man holds his true feelings inside and acts tough and confident.

Dad, I forgive you for these two big mistakes. I know you didn't do them on purpose. But they have cost me a lot in my relationships. I forgive you for not being a spiritual leader and for stuffing your emotions.

Now it's time for part B. It's pretty obvious, Sharon, what the transfer to you and our marriage is. I have not been the spiritual leader in our marriage. Like Dad, I have forced you to lead in this area. I know I have hurt you and I have not earned your respect.

Also, I have transferred from Dad my pattern of not opening up to you in conversations. I have avoided

119

talks with you, and when we do talk, I don't share my
feelings or much of anything personal.
    I know I need to break these patterns.
    Love,
    Steve

Sharon's Letter to Her Dad

Dear Dad,
    As I look back on my childhood with you, I see good
and bad. The good is a dad who loved me and helped
build a stable home and family. The bad is a dad who
didn't work hard enough to build a close relationship
with his daughter.
    Dad, I never felt close to you. You showed me very
little affection, especially once I entered middle school.
I needed your hugs and kisses, but I rarely got any. You
didn't say to me, "You're beautiful."
    I was very hurt, crushed may be a better word, by your
lack of physical affection. I believed I was ugly because
you didn't want to touch me or tell me I was attractive.
    Dad, you also didn't work very hard at building a
good relationship with me. You spent very little one-on-
one time with me. We didn't do things together, just the
two of us. We didn't talk about personal things. You
didn't show much interest in me and my life.
    You spent a lot of time with my brother. Playing
sports, watching sports, watching guy movies together.
It was all about him, and I got left out. I know you felt
more comfortable doing guy things, but that left me out
in the cold.
    Dad, I felt rejected by you. I felt like I wasn't
important to you or interesting enough to attract your
attention and time. I needed your attention and to have
a close relationship with you, but it never happened. I

was very sad and frustrated. Angry, too, underneath, but I never told anyone.

You taught me that physical affection and touch aren't important. You taught me that I was unattractive and not too interesting to men. You taught me to feel anger and disappointment whenever a man doesn't meet my needs. And one more thing: You taught me that the only way to get noticed and get some approval is to perform well at some task. I remember you praised me and were pleased when I got excellent grades and when I completed all my chores.

Dad, I forgive you for these mistakes. I know you didn't do them maliciously. You didn't have a clue about how you were affecting me. I forgive you for hurting me and causing me pain in these areas.

Steve, here's my part B. My dad's lack of physical affection has made me uncomfortable with the whole area of touch and sex. This is one reason I avoid it with you. I don't feel confident with my body. I think I feel you'll be disappointed with me physically, like my dad was.

My lack of emotional closeness with Dad has certainly transferred to you. It has made me want closeness with you very, very badly. When I don't get it, my dad pain rises up and I get way too upset. I'm angry on the surface, but inside I'm hurt.

Because I want and need emotional intimacy, I pressure you and nag you for it. I could not get it with Dad, but I'm going to get it with you no matter what I have to do! Of course, my aggressive approach guarantees I won't get it. When you back off, I get even more angry and resentful at you.

Well, I think I'm getting a picture of why I do some of the things I do with you. I hope figuring out this transfer will help me change these negative behaviors.

Love,

Sharon

Steve's Letter to His Mom

Dear Mom,

This feels strange and disloyal, because you're my mom and you've been a good mom to me. But I have to be honest about a few of your weaknesses that still affect me today in my marriage.

Mom, too many times you pressured me to talk. After school, you'd pepper me to tell you personal things about my day. I can remember you getting very upset with me when I refused to tell you anything. You'd say, in a loud and angry voice, "I just want to know what you're thinking and feeling!" "Talk to me; I want to help you!"

You'd go after me particularly hard when you knew I was upset about something. I'd tell you nothing was wrong or I didn't want to talk about it, and those responses would make you pry all the more.

Mom, your style of pressuring me made me angry and frustrated. I felt like you were trying to control me. The harder you tried to get me to open up, the more I'd clam up. I guess, looking back, you couldn't get Dad to talk so you were trying to get the other man in the house—me—to talk.

You taught me to be defensive and clam up tight when a woman pressures me to talk.

The second big mistake you made was spoiling me. You did everything for me—food, laundry, cleaning up my messes, chores—and never complained. You seemed to enjoy doing it all and didn't ever ask me to do anything. I did a few piddly chores, but that was it. I was treated like a prince.

Mom, you taught me that the woman ought to do all the work in the home. She should serve the man and enjoy it. That has not helped me in my marriage to Sharon.

122

Mom, I forgive you for these mistakes. I know you meant well.

Sharon, here's my part B. I learned to shut down when Mom wanted to talk, and I've done the same thing to you. Many, many times. It's an automatic reaction and I'm a master at it. I need to realize that, just like my mom wanted, all you want is a closer relationship with me.

I can see now why I do so little around the house. I figure it's all your job. My mom did it all! Well, it's time to grow up and do my share of the chores. It's not only the right thing to do, but I know it'll make you happier and our marriage better.

Love,
Steve

Sharon's Letter to Her Ex-Husband

Dear Keith,

I've got some things to say to you that I should have said a long time ago. Our relationship was so full of pain that I just wanted to forget about it and move on. Well, I haven't moved on. The painful things you did to me still control too much of my life.

When we were dating, you pressured me to have sex. I resisted for a while, but eventually I gave in. I thought we were in love and would be married, so it'd be okay. I was wrong. I felt terrible guilt and shame. Our relationship became all about sex, and we didn't develop solid communication. Or spiritual intimacy.

I was angry—and I'm still angry—at myself and at you for the premarital sex. We broke God's law, and I paid a huge price. I've been messed up sexually ever since.

Then, Keith, you dumped me a year into our relationship. I was absolutely stunned and crushed.

*I sobbed and sobbed for days after you told me you
wanted to date other girls. Other girls! I was your girl! I
was giving you my body! We were going to get married
and live together forever!*

*You broke my heart. I was devastated. I begged you
and begged you to take me back. You did, but I wish
you hadn't. I'm embarrassed to think how pathetic I
was back then. Even though we "seemed" to get over it
and we got married, we were never the same. At least, I
wasn't.*

*Keith, I learned from you that I could never trust
a man. Also, I could never give myself fully—in any
way—to a man. I couldn't take the chance that I'd get
so completely rejected again.*

*In our marriage, sex was always about you. Never
about me. When you wanted sex, I provided it. It met
your needs but not my needs. Because I didn't trust you,
I was not a very responsive sexual partner. For me, it
was another chore.*

*You wanted me to do weird, kinky things in bed.
You said you wanted to spice up our sex life. I felt like a
whore. Again, you were thinking of yourself. I did a few
of the behaviors you suggested; afterward, I felt dirty
and worthless.*

*And then I discovered your computer porn problem.
When I realized the kind of websites you were going
to, I was disgusted. Physically ill. And deeply hurt. And
rejected—again. You blamed me! It was not my fault. It
was your fault.*

*Keith, I also learned from you that men are selfish
and will never make any real effort to meet my needs.
You taught me, and I willingly went along and believed
it, that sex is only for the man. I'm only useful for sex
and will never be loved for who I am—for all of me.*

*Finally, you shut me out emotionally. It was me
and my dad all over again. I tried to get you to open*

up and talk, but you weren't interested. The sports on television, the newspaper, a book, the dumb computer, your workshop, your guy friends—everything and everybody was more important than talking to me.

I learned from you that I will never have a close, personal relationship with a man. Which makes me want and need it all the more.

Keith, I forgive you for all that you did to me that hurt me. And you did hurt me, badly. I have been angry and bitter at you for years. I think I hold on to my bitterness to protect myself. But it doesn't protect me. It just keeps on hurting me, and hurting Steve.

So I let all that you did to me go. I forgive you. I release all the hurts to God. I need to truly move on and start fresh with Steve.

Steve, here's what transfers from my ex to you. The sex part is obvious. My guilt and shame from sex before marriage and my feelings of rejection and being used sexually without love have all transferred to you. I don't trust you, and I can't give myself fully to you—emotionally, spiritually, or sexually. I think you'll never love me for me. So when you want sex, all this stuff gets triggered and I put up my wall. I see you as selfish, just like Keith. But that's not right, and it's not fair. You aren't Keith, and I need to give you a chance to prove it.

When you shut me out emotionally and won't talk with me, my Keith issues pop up. I get way too angry at you because I am so tired of men clamming up on me. My reaction is so intense, though, that it pushes you away. How ironic. That's the last thing I want.

I need to lessen my nagging and anger so you'll have a better chance to respond to my requests for personal conversation. With the transfer gone, I think I can approach you in a much better way.

Love,
Sharon

It's All Starting to Make Sense

As Steve and Sharon read their Past Pain Transfer Letters, the light began to dawn. They had already identified—in their Letters of Responsibility—their main mistakes in the marriage. Now they could see how their experiences in past relationships created and continued to sustain their mistakes.

They were determined to cut off the transfer so they could build new, healthy patterns in their marriage. Reading their letters at the end of Week 7 helped. Their Follow-Up Talks in Week 8 would finish the job.

The Follow-Up Talks

To give you a clear picture of how I want you to handle a Follow-Up Talk, here is a portion of Steve and Sharon's dialogue about her letter to her ex-husband:

> Steve: I have read your ex letter three times, Sharon. I remember you telling me before we got married about having sex with him, but I had no idea how painful it was for you. I'm sorry you had to feel so ashamed and guilty and rejected.
>
> Sharon: It was one of the worst experiences of my life. I don't think I've ever gotten over it.
>
> Steve: I want you to heal from it. We all make mistakes, and God has provided forgiveness for us. I hope you can forgive yourself.
>
> Sharon: I think I'm on my way to forgiving myself. I've been carrying the pain around for too long.
>
> Steve: I can now understand why you have a problem enjoying physical affection and sex. I thought it was because you didn't like sex, didn't find me attractive, or were paying me back for some mistakes I'd made.

Now I get it. You've got to feel safe and loved before you can give yourself to me.

Sharon: I'm sorry for all the times I've rejected you physically. I couldn't seem to stop it. It helps to know why I was doing it. I was blaming you for my lack of physical desire. Of course, it was partly you—but it was also coming from my dad and my ex.

Steve: I know I'm partly to blame. My selfishness and not making time to talk—really talk—with you has caused a lot of our problems. I don't want to be like your dad and your ex. I want to be the one guy who will open up to you. I think the talk times we've been having are making a difference. I also want to be the one guy who can approach you gently for physical intimacy and meet your sexual needs.

Sharon: I want you to be that guy. Look, I want to make sure I clean out all my pain with my ex. I've been thinking about my letter to him, and I want to talk more about his dumping me and my begging to get him back. I'm still feeling a lot of anger about that. Can you listen?

Steve: Sure. Go ahead. Take all the time you need to get it out.

Do you see how this works? These Letters expose your past pain, your ineffective learned behaviors, and the transfer to your spouse. The Letters also begin a process of healing your past pain and eliminating all transfer to your spouse. The Follow-Up Talks complete this process and bring you much closer as a couple. Healing together wipes out the transfer *and* connects you on a deeper, more intimate level.

Homework: Weeks 7 and 8

1. Continue to work on improving your relationship with the Lord, stay in contact with your accountability partner, have your four Couple Talk Times per week, go out on one playful date, hold hands, give once-a-day massages, and hug and kiss twice a day.

2. Within six days, each of you write your Past Pain Transfer Letters. Pray before writing that God will guide you and give you what you need to put on paper. Each Letter will include two parts:

Part A
- Honest expression of the pain the person caused you
- What this person taught you about relationships
- Words of forgiveness

Part B
- A description of how your pain and learned behaviors with this person transfer to your spouse

3. Read your Past Pain Transfer Letters at the end of Week 7. The husband reads his Letter first in each session. When your spouse finishes reading a Letter, make some positive and encouraging comments.

4. When all the Letters are read, give your spouse your Letters. Read your spouse's letters several times to prepare for your Follow-Up Talks.

5. During Week 8, have four Follow-Up Talks about your Letters. You can take 15-20 minutes out of your regularly scheduled Couple Talk Times to have these Follow-Up Talks. Discuss the Letters and work to show one another understanding and empathy.

10

Forgive Each Other

"I forgive you." Three simple words that are beautiful, powerful, and healing. Three words that are vitally important to the Change Your Marriage journey. If you don't genuinely forgive your spouse, you can't start fresh and build a new marriage.

Forgiveness is the intellectual, emotional, and spiritual process of completely releasing all your resentments toward someone for the harm that person has done to you.

It's easy to state that forgiveness is a critical component of your new marriage. It's even easy to define forgiveness. What's not easy is actually doing the work of forgiving your spouse. The wounds of a spouse go deep. Your mate, that human person closest to you, can cause more damage than anyone else.

What the Experts Say

So the big question is: "How do you forgive your spouse?" Here's where it gets confusing. The "experts" on forgiveness offer a variety of very different answers.

Some experts say you don't need to forgive. If your spouse has harmed you in a serious way, it's unhealthy to forgive. It's weak and hypocritical to let your spouse off the hook. Hang on to your anger and resentment, because that will keep you safe from your spouse and anyone else who may take advantage of you. Since you'll never be able to trust your spouse again, go ahead and get a divorce. It's better to start over with someone who hasn't hurt you so badly.

Other experts say you need to forgive, and it is an intellectual decision. A choice. An act of the will. Your emotions, which you can't trust anyway, have nothing to do with forgiveness. When your negative, bitter thoughts and feelings about your spouse come up, you push them out of your mind and replace them with thoughts of forgiveness. You need to keep choosing to forgive, following this procedure, for as long as necessary.

Still other experts say forgiveness is a spiritual problem with a spiritual solution. All it takes is one heartfelt prayer asking God to heal your pain and provide you with the power to forgive. This prayer will instantly heal you and get rid of all your resentments against your spouse.

The Experts Are Wrong

I disagree with all these experts. There are two critically important reasons to forgive your spouse. First, your lack of forgiveness will eat *you* alive. Your resentments will make you emotionally, physically, and spiritually sick.

Second, your lack of forgiveness will destroy your marriage. Your resentments will remain, fester, and push you away from your spouse. Your resentments will energize every conflict you have with your spouse. Your resentments will kill your love. And it won't take long.

God, who is the only true expert, makes it clear that you must forgive everyone who wrongs you:

Bear with each other and forgive whatever grievances you may have against one another. Forgive as the Lord forgave you.

Colossians 3:13

Forgiving your spouse will be a huge step toward healing—*yourself and, potentially, your marriage.*

Forgiveness does involve a choice, but it also involves your emotions. You are an emotional creature, and your emotions become connected to all of your experiences, both positive and negative. If you don't express your emotions about your spouse's hurtful behavior, you never will be able to forgive.

Finally, forgiveness is not solely a spiritual problem that can be solved quickly with a prayer, or even by faith alone. Forgiveness is a process that must involve your intellect, your emotions, and your spirituality. It takes time. It is difficult. It takes considerable effort. It takes faith in God. There are no shortcuts to forgiving. You have to follow the right steps in the right order.

I know how you can forgive your spouse, and I'm going to teach you exactly how to do it.

The Two Types of Forgiveness

There is Release Forgiveness, and there is Intimacy Forgiveness. Both involve cleaning out all your resentments you hold toward a person. The big difference between these two types of forgiveness is what happens in your relationship with the person you are forgiving.

Release Forgiveness requires no contact with the person you are forgiving. It requires no particular response from the person. And it requires no change in the person. The person may work with you in the process, may respond well to what you have to say, and may make changes in behavior. If the person does none of these things, the relationship will be lousy and maybe even nonexistent. But you can *still* release your resentment, you can forgive, and you can move on without any impact on your life.

Intimacy Forgiveness is the type of forgiveness I'm talking about in Weeks 9 and 10. Intimacy Forgiveness requires in-person, very personal contact with the person you are forgiving. It requires an understanding, kind, and empathetic response from the person. It requires the person to make changes so you are not hurt in the same areas again.

In Intimacy Forgiveness, you release your resentment toward your spouse, *and* you deepen and improve the marriage. You forgive, and at the same time, you create intimacy.

One important caveat before we move into the how-to section. If your spouse has traumatized you with a big-time, damaging sin (adultery, pornography, alcohol, drugs, verbal abuse, terrible financial decisions), you need to read and apply, right now, Chapters 17 through 19. When the two of you have finished that work, you can return to this point and address all of your other hurts.

You're Ready to Forgive Each Other

You're wondering, "Can we really forgive each other in two weeks?" Truthfully, the answer is no. But you can forgive in ten weeks. My forgiveness process is actually ten weeks long. The steps you have taken in the first eight weeks of the Change Your Marriage program have prepared you to close the forgiveness deal in Weeks 9 and 10.

You've been working on strengthening your relationship with God. Only with God's power can you forgive. You've been working on increasing the positive flow in your marriage: Couple Talk Times, Compliments, Communication Skills, Prayer Together, and Playing and Touching in Romantic Ways.

You've been practicing your new Conflict-Resolving Skills: One at a Time, Speaker and Listener Roles, and Understanding Your Spouse's Feelings and Point of View. You've forgiven those in your past who have hurt you, thereby eliminating the transfer of this pain to your spouse.

The two of you have come a long way, haven't you? You've learned and practiced many new relationship skills, and you are closer as a couple. It's very likely that your resentments against each other have softened and don't seem as important and intense as they once did.

Trust me, though, you still need to go through these two weeks of specific forgiveness steps. You need to make sure that all your resentments are gone. Plus, these forgiveness steps will connect the two of you on a deeper level. When you do forgiveness right, it creates a powerful bond of intimacy.

Week 9

The Letters of Forgiveness

I don't think you'll be shocked at what I'm about to tell you. You have more writing to do. In Week 9, you each will write a Letter of Forgiveness to your spouse. These Letters will be painful to write, but healing.

Take five to seven days in Week 9 and write a Letter that covers all the significant hurts your spouse has caused you during the course of your entire relationship, from the day you met until now. Don't hold back. Don't minimize. Don't sugarcoat. Don't make any excuses for your spouse. Put the truth down on paper in an honest, direct, and detailed way.

Your Letter won't contain any positives. You don't have to forgive your partner for positive, loving behaviors. *The only positive part of the Letter, and it's a big positive, is that you are forgiving your spouse for all the hurts and disappointments he or she has caused you.*

If in doubt, write more and not less. You can't afford to miss anything significant. Be very specific and detailed about what happened and how you felt about it. Describe particular events and patterns of behavior. Relive these painful memories and the emotions connected to them.

Keep in mind that you are doing this assignment only in order to forgive your spouse. In no way are you attempting to score points or build a case that your spouse is more at fault for your marital problems.

Follow this procedure: Describe the event or behavior, express the pain and emotions it generated in you, and use words of forgiveness. This is what you did or said, here's how it impacted me, and I forgive you for it.

These Letters will be longer than your Past Pain Transfer Letters. For most of my clients, it's a five- or six-page Letter. It could be shorter or longer. Pray before you start that God will guide you, give you the right words, and provide the power to forgive.

Week 10

Read and Follow-Up Talks

Your Letters of Forgiveness will be finished by Friday night of Week 9. On Saturday, the beginning of Week 10, the husband will read his Letter out loud to his wife in a private, quiet place in the home. Set aside at least thirty minutes for the reading.

For the next few days, Saturday through Tuesday, the focus will be on the husband's Letter and his resentments. After he reads his Letter, the two of you will have three to four Follow-Up Talks. As you did with your Past Pain Transfer Letters, you can carve out fifteen to twenty minutes from your Couple Talk Times for these Follow-Up Talks.

By Tuesday evening, the husband's process of healing is completed, and it's the wife's turn. She will read her Letter of Forgiveness on Wednesday and then the two of you will have three or four Follow-Up Talks through Saturday. This One at a Time procedure ensures that each spouse's hurts receive full attention and understanding.

Let me walk you through the process.

As you sit down on Saturday, one of you prays out loud that God will use this process to heal and improve your marriage. The husband then reads his Letter of Forgiveness. The wife listens closely and, after he's finished, makes some positive and supportive comments:

"That was difficult to hear but honest."
"I didn't realize how much I'd hurt you in some of those areas."
"I'm sorry for causing you pain."

The husband gives a copy of his Letter to his wife. She will read it several times in an effort to more fully understand and feel his pain. These readings by her will prepare her for the Follow-Up Talks.

It is essential that the wife (the listening spouse) completely and unconditionally accepts what the husband (the reading spouse) states in his Letter and in the Follow-Up Talks. She must believe he is telling the truth. He has an absolute right to his truth, his point of view, and his feelings about her behavior.

She cannot get defensive, argumentative, or critical at any point in the process. If she is unable to be 100 percent understanding and supportive, there will be no Intimacy Forgiveness, and more damage will be done to the marriage. He will know she doesn't "get it," and now it will take longer to heal and forgive.

Before each Follow-Up Talk, pray something like this: "God, help us talk about these painful things so we can heal, forgive, and get closer as a couple." The husband brings up certain parts of his Letter (key events, memories, patterns of behavior, and his emotions at the time) and talks about them.

As he talks, the wife reflects his pain and his emotions and seeks to build understanding. She wants him to realize that she does "get it," that she knows what happened and how he feels about it.

She says she's sorry many times as he tells her what she did to hurt him. She offers no excuses or rationalizations for her behavior. No "Yeah, but . . ." statements come out of her mouth. She doesn't blame him or anyone else for her hurtful actions.

If she slips and gets defensive and starts to argue over his version of events, he is allowed to point out her mistake and call for a break. After a ten- or fifteen-minute cooling off period, they come back together. She apologizes for her mistake and asks him to forgive her, and they pick up where they left off.

The wife can share why she thinks she did the hurtful behaviors. In no way is she permitted to excuse her behavior. Rather, she is trying to explain what happened. If she can figure out where she went wrong—in her thinking, her expression of emotion, her spiritual life, her mishandling of stress, and her incorrect assumptions—it will help her correct these behaviors.

In the reading of his Letter and in the Follow-Up Talks, the hurts he covers will also be the behaviors his wife must change. His hurts will highlight his needs. He is forgiving and also pointing out his needs.

As the husband cleans out his hurts, he brings up specific behaviors he needs his wife to change. "Honey, you angered and hurt me so many times by criticizing me instead of praising me. I really need you to reduce the critical comments and praise me for at least one thing every day."

The wife responds to his requests for change with understanding and a commitment to meet his needs. "I'm sorry for being so critical. I know now how much damage I did with those kinds of negative comments. I will work hard to compliment you at least once a day. I'll be softer and kinder in how I approach you."

By Tuesday night, the husband's "turn" is over. The reading of his Letter and the three or four Follow-Up Talks have created understanding, produced forgiveness, highlighted his needs, and brought them closer as a couple.

Now, they switch roles, and from Wednesday to Saturday the wife will read her Letter and they'll have the Follow-Up Talks.

To illustrate Weeks 9 and 10, let's take a look at how Steve and Sharon handled these Change Your Marriage steps. Your homework is found at the end of Chapter 11.

11

"I Forgive You"

One Couple's Journey
through Weeks 9 and 10

Did you ever decide to do something that you really didn't want to do? Really, really, really didn't want to do? You fully expected the experience to be a nightmare. But then you actually had a terrific time and were very glad you did it?

Recently, I had such an experience. My thirteen-year-old son, William, and I are part of a father-son group at Oakwood Community Church in Tampa. Including me, there are eight fathers in the group: Dave Conner, Doug Cress, Scott Russel, Kyle MacCullough, Randall Huber, Craig Hickson, and Pete Kluck.

Part of the group's purpose is to do activities together as fathers and sons. We want to build relationships and teach our sons how to be healthy, godly men. The fathers decided that our first big activity would be a weekend camping trip. I had only one problem with that: I hate camping. *Loathe* may be a better word.

I love outdoor activities. William and I have played all kinds of sports outside for years. I love to hike, too. But at night, I want to be indoors and take a shower and have my creature comforts. When I go on a trip, I'm a hotel kind of guy. If God had meant for us to sleep outside, he wouldn't have created hotels.

I've been camping, and I can't quite figure out why I hate it so much. Maybe it's the sleeping in a tent on the lumpy ground. Actually, there is no sleeping. There is lying awake all night. Maybe it's getting bitten by fleas, ticks, fire ants, flies, disease-carrying mosquitoes, bees, wasps, and a host of other flying pests. Maybe it's the nasty bug spray, which not only stinks to high heaven but actually seems to attract bugs.

Maybe it's the cruel reality that no matter where you sit around the fire, the smoke will blow into your face.

Even after I told the guys my reasons, they still wanted Will and me to go. They didn't understand my animosity toward camping because all seven of them are camping enthusiasts. They had the tents, the grills, the cooking utensils, the folding chairs, and every conceivable accessory.

I realized with horror that I had joined a group of bona fide mountain men. These guys had all the camping skills down cold. They could put up a tent in five minutes, cook over an open fire, rig a hammock, fix any piece of equipment, kill wildlife and prepare the meat, and whittle sticks into the shapes of forest animals.

They shared stories of many past camping trips and the assorted disasters that had occurred: animal attacks, running out of water, getting hopelessly lost in the middle of nowhere, terrible storms, lightning strikes. . . . They weren't building my confidence.

But I liked these guys and wanted to build some meaningful memories with Will. So I sucked it up and we went on the camping trip. The fact that Will and I were able to sleep in a cabin on the property made the decision easier.

Much to my surprise, Will and I had a fantastic time. All the things about camping I didn't like did happen, but it didn't make any difference. Will and I bonded with each other and with the other guys and their sons. We played together, ate together, did a service project together, and had a very meaningful "entering manhood ceremony" one night.

I dreaded that camping trip, but Will and I will never forget it. It made a difference in our lives and in our relationship.

This forgiveness process is a lot more difficult and painful than our camping trip, and certainly something you don't want to do. But the result is going to be the same. It will be good for you both. It will lead to changes in each of you and in your marriage.

Sharon's Letter of Forgiveness

Dear Steve,

This is not going to be pleasant. In fact, I hate doing it. I'm going to dredge up a lot of painful memories. Some of my hurts won't surprise you, but some of them will. I know this is necessary so that I can clean out all my resentments of you and forgive you. This will, I hope and pray, help us move forward in a new relationship.

When I think about finding out about your contact with your ex-girlfriend, it still hurts. How could you? We were in a serious, committed relationship! I'd given my heart to you! Only to discover that you were talking with her, were emailing back and forth, and even had lunch with her a few times.

I can remember that night we talked about it in your car, parked by my apartment. As you told me the story, I felt nauseated. I was crushed and furious and unbelievably hurt all at the same time. We didn't talk about it much after that night, and I wish we had. You were sorry and it seemed to go away, but it really didn't go away. I lost my trust in you that night and never got it all back.

Steve, it's time for me to let it go. I want and need to trust you. I forgive you for having contact with that girl.

The miscarriage I had with our first child was a terrible blow for me. All my hopes were dashed when I lost that precious child. But what made it worse was your reaction. Or lack of reaction, I should say. You didn't show any emotion. You went with me to the hospital, but you seemed distant from me.

I was desperate to talk about it, to vent my feelings of anguish and grief, but you refused to talk about it. You clammed up when I needed you the most. I know it hurt you, too, but you just wanted to move on. I was so frustrated and hurt by your response. This was your baby, too!

Not only did you refuse to listen to my feelings, but you wouldn't share your feelings with me. What did you feel? What did you think? I never knew. And I needed to know.

You thought having another baby would solve the problem and take away my pain. It didn't. I love our daughter dearly and am so happy she came into our family. But she didn't replace the child I lost. That we lost.

Steve, I forgive you for not being there for me when I had the miscarriage. I know you didn't mean to hurt me, but you did. I'm releasing my resentments over your reaction.

Your decisions in so many areas, without my input, caused me a great deal of anger. When I found out about each decision, I felt worthless to you. Like I didn't matter. I wanted us to be a team, but I was left on the bench. Remember when you took that promotion and we had to move fifteen hundred miles? I couldn't believe you took the job and then informed me. It probably was the right decision for the family, but you robbed me of the right to make that decision with you. I mean, it obviously impacted my life, too!

Steve, I forgive you for that job decision and all the decisions you've made without me. I don't want to harbor any bitterness at you for these mistakes.

Your workaholism has caused me a lot of pain over the years. All your broken promises to me and the kids have taken a toll on my respect for you. And my trust. You lied to me so many times, telling me you'd cut back and be home more. Telling me that in just a few months things would lighten up and you'd have more time to be at home. Of course, it never happened.

On our tenth anniversary, you were late coming home from work, and we had to cancel our special dinner reservation. It was an awful night when it should have been a joyful night.

I was mad at you for lying and mad at myself for believing your lies. My anger and sense of betrayal made me pull away from you. I was increasingly cold to you as I built my own life with the kids, my friends, my job, and my church activities.

I forgive you for your workaholism and all the lies that have gone with it.

You have not been the spiritual leader—for our marriage or our family. Seeing you avoid this important job has wounded me deeply. You have not prayed with me regularly. We have not read the Bible together but a handful of times. We have not talked about our individual spiritual lives. You have not led our family in devotions more than a dozen times over the years.

You would start leading spiritually, but then all too soon stop. I have lost respect for you because of this. A lot of respect. I didn't have a spiritual leader in my dad, so I wanted one in you. No, I needed one in you.

I forgive you, Steve, for failing to step up and be my spiritual leader. I still need you to do it, and I'm

*cautiously optimistic because in recent weeks you have
started to lead. I'm letting go of all my resentments in
this area.*

*One of my big resentments has been your lack of
help with the chores, the housework, and the kids.
Your being at work so much was a part of that, I know.
When you aren't home, you can't do anything for me.
But even when you were home, you did very little. And
when you did a small job, you expected me to gush all
over you with praise.*

*Not getting help has made me angry, massively
frustrated, resentful, and exhausted. I felt like a single
parent because I was doing it all. I hate being a nagging
witch, but that's what it took to get you to do chores.*

*Your ignoring the kids or spending the minimum
amount of time with them has hurt me so very much.
I see them get hurt and their self-esteem suffer because
Dad's job and Dad's television shows and Dad's
computer time is more important than they are. As a
mom, when my kids get hurt, I get hurt.*

*Steve, I forgive you for not doing your share of the
chores and for not being an involved dad with the kids.
It's hard to let this resentment go, but I do. The steps
you've made recently with chores and spending time
with the kids give me some hope.*

*A major area of resentment, Steve, is your clamming
up and not talking with me on a personal level. You
have, until lately, successfully resisted all my efforts to
have regular talk times. You've always said, "I'm too
busy," "This isn't a good time," "I don't want to talk
about that," or "I'm too tired."*

*I want and need you to listen, really listen, to me
when I talk. I want you to understand me and what's
going on in my life. I need you to open up and share
with me your thoughts, your feelings, and what's going
on in your life. That's why we're married—to be close!*

I have had a deep sadness and hopelessness about our superficial communication. When I get shut out by you, it makes me feel as if I'm not important enough for you to share personal things. I feel unfulfilled and I despair about our marriage.

Steve, I forgive you for shutting me out in the communication area. I've enjoyed our talk times these last few weeks and pray we continue to make time to talk and learn to talk on a deeper level.

Steve, I have resented your pressuring me for sex throughout our marriage. You complain I'm never in the mood. You want to know why? Because you don't meet my need for emotional intimacy and don't help me with the chores and the kids. So later in the evening when you want sex, I'm tired and resentful, and sex is the last thing I want.

Remember our weekend in the mountains last summer? I wanted to talk and rekindle our love by having fun together. I pictured intimate breakfasts, long walks in the woods, and candlelight dinners. You slept in, watched television, and wanted sex twice a day.

Steve, when I don't feel close to you, sex is nothing but a chore. I feel used and cheap. And then angry that I gave in to you. And, speaking about sex, you're way too fast.

There's no talking before, foreplay lasts only until you're ready, and then it's all over in fifteen minutes. How about me? I'm not ready, I'm not aroused, and I have no chance for an orgasm. I am so frustrated afterward!

I forgive you, Steve, for your mistakes in our sexual relationship. I release all my resentments of you pressuring me and not preparing me for sex.

Steve, I forgive you for all these things. It was a lot to write, but I want to get everything out. I believe we can start fresh and build a new marriage.

Love,
Sharon

146

It's All Cleaned Out

Sharon's Letter was long, wasn't it? But, it was honest and complete. She obviously took to heart my advice: If in doubt, write more and not less. Her Letter also packed quite a gigantic emotional punch. She didn't hold back. She shared her emotions freely and fully.

If she had written this Letter even two weeks earlier, it would have been much nastier and more intense. The steps she and Steve completed in Weeks 1 through 8 connected them in some positive ways and took the edge off her pain with Steve. She still had her resentments toward him, but they were now at manageable levels and could be completely cleaned out of her system.

Sharon used words of forgiveness in her Letter, and she meant them. Reading her Letter out loud to Steve was a further step toward forgiveness. But it took the Follow-Up Talks to make her forgiveness real. Their dialogue about parts of her Letter—in particular, Steve's healing responses—led to four important results:

1. Full Release Forgiveness was achieved.
2. A major step toward Intimacy Forgiveness was accomplished.
3. Key communication skills were learned.
4. Tangible, meaningful closeness was gained.

I've included below two portions of their Follow-Up Talks to show you how to make these dialogues successful.

The Follow-Up Talks

Sharon: I want to talk through my miscarriage. It's important that you understand the pain I went through. If you can share my pain and walk with me through what happened, I feel like the loss won't separate us anymore.

Steve: Talk about it as long as you need to. I'll listen and do my best to understand what you went through.

Sharon: The worst part, the absolute worst, was the operation to clean everything out. I was lying there, and instead of getting a baby, what was left of my baby was being taken out of me.

Steve: That must have been awful. I can't even imagine your feelings. I know you wanted that child so much. So did I.

Sharon: I did want our baby, desperately. All my hopes and dreams were destroyed that day. I felt like God had turned his back on me and was punishing me. I was angry with him for doing this to me.

Steve: I was angry at God, too. I mean, he knew how losing the baby would crush you, but he allowed it anyway. Why? I'm sorry for how bad it was for you. And I'm sorry I was a jerk and wasn't there for you when you needed me so much.

Sharon: You just sat there in the hospital room, staring at the wall, and saying nothing. That hurt me and made me feel like I was alone. And that you didn't care.

Steve: I did care, but I'm sorry I couldn't say something to help you. I was angry at God and angry at myself for not being able to help. I couldn't do anything to make it better. I felt totally useless and helpless. I tried to tell myself it wasn't really a baby, but that was a lie.

Sharon: I was so angry at you for not comforting me. It helps to know what you were thinking and feeling back then. I thought you didn't care about me or the baby. . . .

❦

Sharon: I married you because I loved you and wanted to get closer and closer to you. I wanted you to talk to me and tell me personal things you didn't share with anyone else. Instead, you have stayed on the surface with me. We haven't had regular conversation times, you haven't been a good listener, and you haven't shared what you're really thinking and feeling.

Steve: It's true, and I'm sorry. I haven't been comfortable with the whole personal conversation thing. I love you, but I don't know how to talk to you. I automatically clam up whenever you ask me to open up and share something personal. There's no excuse for it, and I need to change.

Sharon: I can't live the old way anymore. I'm sick of it. It hurts me too badly. If we don't talk and connect on a deeper level on a regular basis, we'll never have much of a marriage.

Steve: I agree. I've finally figured out that my holding everything inside hurt me as well as you. I can learn how to open up.

Sharon: Let's keep having the Talk Times four times a week. I think they're starting to work. I can feel my love for you coming back. And let's try my idea of you helping with the chores and kids, us having a good Talk Time, and then making love.

Steve: It's a deal. I'll keep working on telling you what's going on with me. It goes against my natural style, but I know it's important to you and to us. And I finally get it: I have to do my share around the house and talk to you to get you ready for our physical times.

As you see in Sharon's Letter of Forgiveness and these brief dialogues, she and Steve are talking about needs. In fact, needs—their importance, what happens when they go unmet in a marriage, and the expression of needs to one another—have been a central underlying theme these past ten weeks. Now, in our final two weeks, we'll focus directly on this critical area.

Homework: Weeks 9 and 10

1. Continue to work on improving your relationship with the Lord, stay in contact with your accountability partner, have your four Couple Talk Times per week, go out on one playful date, hold hands, give once-a-day massages, and hug and kiss twice a day.
2. Within seven days, each of you write a Letter of Forgiveness to your spouse. Pray before writing that God will give you the memories and the emotions you need to put on paper. Your Letters will include three points for each resentment:
   - Here's what happened
   - Here's how it impacted me (my pain and emotions)
   - I forgive you
3. At the beginning of Week 10, the husband reads his Letter out loud to his wife. She makes some positive, supportive comments. She also reads and rereads his Letter several times to prepare for the Follow-Up Talks. The wife must believe and accept that her husband's Letter is the truth.
4. The husband and wife have three to four Follow-Up Talks about his Letter. By Tuesday evening, they've completed their work on his Letter.
5. Beginning on Wednesday of Week 10, the roles are reversed. The wife reads her Letter of Forgiveness, and they have the Follow-Up Talks.

12

The Code Queen and the Clam

We've arrived at the last two weeks in the Change Your Marriage program. All the work you've done in the previous ten weeks has prepared you for this final step in building a brand-new, successful marriage: Meet Your Deepest Needs.

When needs are not met in a marriage, both spouses are unhappy, and there is no intimacy. But on top of that, you and your partner will eventually go to some other person or behavior outside the marriage in a misguided attempt to get your needs met.

It is these outside-the-marriage, often addictive behaviors that ultimately destroy your love.

Why do you think so many spouses are addicted to television, the computer, and video games? They're trying to get their needs met!

Why are so many spouses addicted to work, kids, taking care of the home, alcohol, drugs, and gambling? They're trying to get their needs met!

Why are so many spouses addicted to pornography and having affairs? They're trying to get their needs met!

These addictions don't meet any needs, and they seriously damage you and your marriage. Long-standing, entrenched addictions must be treated professionally *as* addictions.

The stakes are high, aren't they? To avoid certain disaster and to create a new and vibrant intimacy, you must meet each other's needs.

You're Way Past Square One

The truth is, you have been identifying and meeting each other's needs throughout the Change Your Marriage program. Your regular Couple Talk Times have given you many opportunities to communicate and a forum to discuss all kinds of needs. Your Top Two and Top Three mistake-correcting behaviors have met your spouse's needs in these areas.

Your Fabulous Fourteen list of compliments met some needs. The addition of Carryover Topics, five-minute Prayer Together, and Prayer to Conversation to your Couple Talk Times has deepened your emotional and spiritual intimacy.

Your romantic moves (watching a romantic movie, going out on playful dates, holding hands, giving massages, and kissing and hugging) have pumped some life into your love and your physical intimacy.

Your new Conflict-Resolving Skills can prevent your disagreements from getting in the way of meeting needs. As a secondary benefit, resolving conflicts the right way often leads to closeness and passion.

Your hard work in cleaning out transfer from your past relationships and forgiving your spouse has removed resentments that were blocking you from meeting your spouse's needs. Your Letters of Forgiveness identified some of your most critical needs. By working together on your past pain, you have also learned how to communicate on a much deeper level.

So the two of you are in good shape in terms of meeting each other's needs. You're already doing it. But my job is to make sure you have needs-meeting down cold.

Because needs are so important to your new marriage, I will use this chapter and the next to close the deal. I want you to have the right information and strategies to continue to meet needs for the rest of your marriage.

In this chapter, I'll cover some key *obstacles* to meeting needs and some practical how-tos. In Chapter 13, I'll focus on meeting needs in the three major areas of intimacy: the emotional, the physical, and the spiritual.

The Code Queen

Wife, you use a special language to communicate your needs to your husband. I call it the *Code*. Other women understand the Code perfectly. Unfortunately, men do not. Your husband has no idea how to crack your Code.

You send messages about your needs that your husband cannot understand. You think you are sending a crystal clear message to your husband about a need. In fact, your message is not crystal clear. It's in Code, and he doesn't know the Code!

He doesn't get the message, so he doesn't meet your need. You get upset, don't you? You're angry and hurt because he didn't meet your need—and because he *knew* what your need was and deliberately chose to not meet it. You blame him, don't you?

The truth is, you need to send a clear message! Here's an example from my marriage.

It's a Saturday morning at the Clarke household. It's about nine o'clock and I'm working at my desk, paying bills for the four sleeping kids upstairs. Sandy comes up to me and says: "Dave, I'm going out for a while. I've got to get some groceries and some shoes for the girls. I'm behind on the laundry, and I have no idea what we're going to have for dinner."

I reply: "Okay, honey. See you later." We kiss, and Sandy leaves. The only thing I'm thinking is, "I hope she comes up with an idea for dinner."

Sandy *thinks* she said: "Dave, I'm tired and stressed out. Getting groceries and shoes is all I want to do today. Please do a load or two of laundry and come up with some plan for dinner."

Now, let me ask you something. Did she actually say what she thinks she said? No! All you women reading this are thinking, "Yes, she did ask you to do some laundry and make dinner plans." No, she didn't! She used the *Code*! What are the chances I'm going to crack her Code and get her real message? Zero!

You know the rest of the story. Sandy gets home and has a fit because I've done no laundry and have no ideas about dinner. And it's all my fault! I'm telling you, it's not my fault! It's Sandy's fault. She didn't send a clear message. She thinks she did, but she didn't.

Here's another example. Sandy asks me, "Do you want to go to the party Friday night?" This is a straightforward question requiring a yes or no answer. Right? As a man, that's how I take it. I don't pick up a vibe or a hidden message of any kind.

I say, "No. I don't want to go." Neat and clean. Question answered, and we can move on. Not quite. Sandy gets upset! She says, in a slightly elevated voice: "No? What do you mean, no? You know I want to go to the party! I've been talking about it for two weeks! I'm hurt that you don't want to take me!"

I'm thinking two things. First, my dream of a beautiful, romantic evening just went down the tubes. Second, how am I supposed to know she wanted to go to the party?

Sandy is convinced she said, "I want to go to the party Friday night. Would you take me?" But she didn't say that. She used the Code. I don't know the Code!

Wife, forget hints. Forget subtlety of any kind! You aren't dealing with a sensitive, perceptive, intuitive man. Somebody else married that guy. You're dealing with a logical, black-and-white man who wouldn't recognize a nuance if it came equipped with a neon light and a siren. Your husband requires a shovel to the head—conversationally speaking.

Your job is to tell your man in clear, direct words exactly *what* you need and exactly *when* you want the behavior accomplished.

The Clam

Husband, you have your own set of problems when it comes to getting your real needs met by your wife. You have a deep need to be emotionally connected to your wife. You have a deep need to be spiritually connected to your wife. But you are very uncomfortable with these needs and *clam* up whenever your wife tries to get close to you in these two areas of intimacy.

The Clam keeps everything personal inside: thoughts, feelings, stresses, worries, memories, spiritual life. . . . When your wife asks you to open up and share what's inside, you automatically clam up and respond with defensive maneuvers. You don't want to be vulnerable.

You can trust your wife with your secrets, but you're not certain of that. You don't want to take the chance. You have never seen a man you were close to open up and share deeply with a woman. You never saw your dad do it. You never saw either grandpa do it.

If Dad ever did share himself personally with Mom, it was behind closed doors. You did see your dad stiffen up and resist Mom's attempts at deeper conversation a million times. So you learned from your dad to keep your guard up with a woman.

Clam, you know how this works. After a bad day at work, you will arrive and make a beeline for your wife. You'll say,

"Honey, I had a bad day and need to pour out my heart to you!" Is this what you do? Are you kidding? Never! You won't appear out of control or weak or vulnerable.

When your wife asks you how your day was, you'll give her one of your classic "I'm avoiding intimacy" replies: "Fine," or "Okay," or "Pretty good." These responses tell her nothing, which is the point. You are a master of sidestepping questions and holding back the personal information and feelings the woman wants.

Your wife knows when something's bothering you. She does have intuition and she's usually right. For all the good it will do her. She asks you: "Is there anything bothering you?" You reply with a lie: "No." She tries again: "What's wrong, honey?" You answer with another lie: "Nothing."

Whenever your wife presses you for personal information, you clam up and give nothing up. "I don't want to talk about it." "Let's talk about it later." "I'm too busy right now." "I'm watching this television show." "I can't even tell you what's on my mind." "I don't know."

Husband, it's time to stop clamming up and resisting your wife's attempts to meet your deeper needs. That's what God brought her into your life to do!

Your job is to start opening up with your wife and being honest about what's inside. Not only will she be thrilled, but your marriage will be so much better.

Make Your Needs Clear

It's the unspoken things that kill a marriage. You both have told each other many personal, difficult, and intimate things in this Change Your Marriage process. Now it's time to speak the truth in the area of needs.

Ask Twice a Day

The only surefire, guaranteed way to identify your spouse's needs is to ask. Don't assume you know. Don't try to read your partner's mind. You'll be wrong, and needs will go unmet. At least twice a day, ask, in person or over the telephone, what his or her needs are.

Ask in the morning, before you go your separate ways: "Honey, what do you really need from me today? What can I do for you?" Husband, because you don't have a memory, jot down your wife's needs. At the beginning of your evening together, when you first see each other, ask for each other's needs again. "Sweetheart, what can I do for you tonight?"

When your spouse asks for your needs, give an honest and specific list of your real needs. Your needs will go from the mundane, routine level to the extremely personal level. Here's the list one wife gave her husband in the morning, after he asked for her needs:

> "Please pick up Susie at 5:30 from her ballet class."
> "Please call the mechanic and schedule my car to go in this Wednesday or Thursday morning."
> "Please take time tonight, in our Couple Talk Time, to talk about your possible job change."
> "Please have a talk with Johnny tonight about his temper."
> "Please make wild, passionate love to me tonight at 9:30."

He'll remember that last one without writing it down! It may be the only one he does remember. Actually, if the husband meets the first four needs on his wife's list, the passionate lovemaking might just happen.

If your spouse forgets to ask you your needs, go ahead and tell him or her your needs.

Once a week, in one of your Talk Times, ask each other: "How am I doing meeting your needs? How can I do better?" Because when needs are not met, your marriage suffers. This once-a-week, need-performance evaluation will keep you on track.

List Your Top Three

In your first Couple Talk Time of Week 11, tell your spouse what your top three needs are. Be honest. Don't hold back. You'll never get your deeper needs met if you don't tell your partner exactly what they are.

As an illustration, here are the top three needs of a couple I recently saw in therapy:

Husband	Wife
1. Physical affection and sex	1. Closeness in conversation
2. Respect	2. Spiritual intimacy
3. Shared activities	3. Romance

Take a few minutes to describe your needs and define precisely what you're talking about. Just giving the general category isn't clear enough. For example, the husband may say: "When I say respect, I mean two things. One, to make me a priority. I want my time with you to be more important than your time with anyone else. I want you and me to have our Talk Times before you call your mother and friends and talk on the phone. If we're talking, I want you to tell the kids to wait until we're done.

"Two, respect means to praise me often—for my character, for how I look, for doing chores, for being a good dad, and for how hard I work at my job."

The wife may say: "By romance, I mean I want you to pursue me and draw me into romantic situations. Get me mushy cards, send me flowers, give me special little surprise gifts, and plan—every other week—romantic dates for us."

Talk about the Obstacles

In your second Couple Talk Time of Week 11, discuss what gets in the way of meeting these needs. Maybe it's the Code. Maybe it's the Clam resisting any personal connection. Maybe you're too focused on the kids and their needs. Maybe you think you aren't able to meet one of your spouse's top needs. Maybe you're afraid to try and fail.

When you talk about the obstacles, you can remove them. When they are exposed, their power is eliminated.

Paint a Picture

In your third and fourth Couple Talk Times of Week 11, paint a picture of each of your Top Three needs. In other words, tell your spouse in clear, direct words how to meet those needs.

The husband who has the need for respect might say: "I need you to praise me at least once a day. You can use any of the categories I described earlier: my character, my body or my clothes, chores, fatherhood, or my job."

The wife who has the need for romance might say: "I'd like a romantic card or letter from you at least twice a month. Be sure to write a paragraph or two about me and why you love me so much."

Of course, this is only a very small piece of the painting-a-picture-of-your-needs process.

These two needs, respect and romance, are very large categories, and there are many ways you can instruct your spouse to meet them in any given week. And that's exactly what you'll do with these needs and all your other deeper needs. Part of building and maintaining a powerful and fresh love is sharing your needs and coming up with a myriad of different ways for your spouse to meet them.

From now on, I want you to continue sharing your needs and telling your spouse in specific terms how to meet them.

Homework: Week 11

1. Continue to work on improving your relationship with the Lord, stay in contact with your accountability partner, have your four Couple Talk Times per week, go out on one playful date, hold hands, give once-a-day massages, and hug and kiss twice a day.
2. Twice a day, in the morning and the evening, ask your spouse what his or her needs are. Jot down the needs and meet them.

3. In your first Couple Talk Time, tell your spouse what your Top Three needs are. Take a few minutes and define what you mean by each need.

4. In your second Couple Talk Time, discuss the obstacles that get in the way of meeting your spouse's needs.

5. In your third and fourth Couple Talk Times, paint a clear picture of your Top Three needs. Tell your spouse, in specific terms, some ways you want each of these needs met. Commit to always sharing your deeper needs and to give your spouse a variety of different ways to meet them.

6. In your fourth Couple Talk Time, ask each other: "How did I do meeting your needs this week? How can I do better?" Commit to asking these questions once a week from now on.

13

To Be Soul Mates,
You Have to Be "Need Mates"

I'm about to write four words that will trigger wildly different responses from my female and male readers. *Hallmark Card television commercials.* The women are thinking: "Oh yes! Those are my all-time favorite commercials." The men are thinking: "Oh no! I'm begging you not to go there."

Women love Hallmark Card commercials. Absolutely love them. Women love these commercials more than the television movie the commercials are sponsoring. When one of these commercials comes on, the women stop talking and lean forward to catch every word. The men suddenly have to go to the bathroom or get another drink.

Recently, I had a conversation about these Hallmark commercials with Sandy and my twenty-three-year-old daughter, Emily. In unison, they cooed: "Ooooooooooh, those commercials are soooooooooooo sweet and beautiful!" Immediately, they began to describe their favorites:

- The young soldier who travels through a terrible snow-storm and joins the family as they're singing a Christmas carol
- The college English professor getting a card from a for-mer student who is now an English teacher herself
- The little girl who gets a card in the mail from her mom
- At the end of a day in which she has done a million things for her two small sons, the mom gets a card from the boys saying thanks

I don't have room for the five or six other favorites they reeled off. Sandy and Emily were laughing and crying as they remembered these special commercials. I sat there with my mouth open, stunned at their outpouring of raw emotion. I said: "Excuse me, but these commercials aren't real. The people and situations are all made up. They just want you to buy cards."

A terrible silence fell over the room. Boy, if looks could kill. They both told me rather snippily, "You just don't get it." I replied: "Oh, I get it all right. I just don't want to break down in tears while watching television."

Believe me, men are not immune to the powerful emo-tional impact of Hallmark Card commercials. Select three of the toughest guys on the planet: an army combat veteran with three Purple Hearts and a Medal of Honor, a cham-pion triathlete, and that mountain climber who gnawed his own arm off to save his life. Sit these guys down on a couch and force them to watch five Hallmark Card commercials in a row.

By the end of the first commercial, they'd be quietly snif-fling. By the middle of the third one, they'd be openly sob-bing. By the fourth one, they'd be crying for their mamas and engaging in a group hug.

Why do women love Hallmark Card commercials? Because these commercials create the very scenes of intimacy women yearn to experience in their own lives. Women are drawn to the expression of tender, heartwarming emotions and personal thoughts. They love to see men and women lower their walls and connect on a deeper level.

Every wife wants and needs Hallmark Card commercial moments with those to whom she is closest in her life. Especially the one person she loves more than anyone else: you, her husband. You don't have to cry your eyes out with your wife. But you do have to regularly share with her your personal, inside thoughts and feelings. You do have to tell her private things you don't tell anyone else.

Meet Your Top Three Needs

You and your spouse have three essential needs: emotional, physical, and spiritual. In the new marriage you're building, you'll be able to meet these needs on a regular basis. When you do, you'll experience intimacy that is deep and personal. Let's take a look at these three needs and some specific, proven ways you can meet them.

Her Number One Need Is Emotional Intimacy

If you're not talking regularly with your wife on a personal level, I have some bad news for you: She doesn't feel loved by you.

The number one desire of your wife's heart is to be close to you. To know you as no one else knows you. To hear you talk honestly and openly about your life, your walk with God, your relationship with her, your children, your work, your hopes and dreams, her life, and the things that are important to her.

She wants you to join her in building a better, closer, and deeper relationship. She understands that what she's asking will be very difficult for you. In fact, it will be one of the most difficult things you have ever done. But she is hoping and praying that you love her enough to do it.

For years, I held back with my wife, Sandy I talked with her only about safe, superficial topics. She tried over and over to get me to lower my wall and let her see what I was really thinking and feeling. But I wouldn't do it. I didn't think she needed to know the personal things about me.

Man, was I wrong. I was hurting her deeply! I was making my precious wife unhappy and unfulfilled in our marriage. It was *my fault*. Hiding behind my wall and holding her at arm's length was squeezing the life out of her and our marriage. We still loved each other, but we weren't feeling or acting in love. The fun, the romance, the exciting sex, and the passion were gone. Maybe that's where you are now.

I finally figured out how to open up and let Sandy see inside. To know the real me. I won't lie to you. It wasn't easy. But it has been worth all the effort. Sandy and I are closer and happier now than we've ever been.

You know what I found out about myself as I worked to meet Sandy's need for emotional intimacy? I discovered that *I* had a deep need for emotional intimacy, too! Husband, you're going to find out the same thing.

How did I learn how to open up and share myself with Sandy? By doing a lot of steps in the last eleven weeks of my Change Your Marriage program. Just as I learned how to emotionally connect with Sandy, you've been learning how to do this with your wife.

Here are two additional "talking" strategies that will accelerate your learning curve in the arena of opening up in conversation with your wife.

The Pad

Prepare for your Couple Talk Times by carrying a notepad with you everywhere you go. Just get one of those small writing notebooks you can find in any drugstore. As you go through your day and things happen to you that you think might interest your wife, jot them down. It might be something that made you feel an emotion like anger, frustration, happiness, or satisfaction. It might be an interaction with another person. It might be something God taught you.

When you get home and meet with your wife in your one-on-one Talk Time, you'll have a little list of things to share with her. Don't trust your memory. You don't have a memory! Your wife remembers everything. You remember nothing. Use the pad.

If you're a technological kind of guy, you can use a PDA, Blackberry, or iPhone to jot down these conversation topics.

I've had many husbands say to me, "Dave, I'll feel like an idiot going around all day with my notepad, and then sitting in front of my wife with it." My response has always been the same: "You'll feel like a bigger idiot when you are sitting in front of your wife with nothing to say."

Share Work Stress

Of all the husbands I've seen in therapy, 99.9 percent have told me, "I leave work at work. I don't talk to my wife about what goes on at my job. Rehashing my work day will make me miserable and stress me out." I'll tell you what I've told these husbands: "Although it is a natural tendency to stuff your work stress, it's not healthy for you or for your marriage. Unless you work for the CIA and have to keep secrets for national security reasons, you need to talk with your wife about problems at work. When you open up to your wife and express your work stress, it lowers your stress level and brings the two of you closer."

Graveyards are filled with husbands who stuffed their work stress and kept it buried in their guts. Sure, they checked out early with heart attacks, strokes, and other deadly, stress-related traumas, but at least they held the line and kept work at work. If you want to live healthier and longer, regularly talk out your work stress with the one person you love and trust more than anyone else on earth.

Not too long ago, I had a husband in my office who finally realized the futility and danger of keeping his work life a secret. This guy had hypertension, chest pains, and headaches from stuffing his job stress of twenty years. He was a heart attack waiting to happen. When he followed my advice and took the risk of sharing his work stress with his wife, do you know what happened? The same thing that's happened with every husband who began sharing with his wife, cleaning his system of work-related strain, tension, and pressure. This man felt relief and a significant reduction in his stress level. His chest pains and headaches went away. He felt better than he had in years.

His wife felt better because she got to know him better. His job was a huge part of his life that he had walled off from her. She wanted and needed to know what was going on at work and the problems he was facing. She couldn't solve his problems, but she could listen and be a valuable source of support and encouragement.

Was their marriage better and closer because of his decision to talk about work? You'd better believe it. He said to me, "Dave, I wish I had done this twenty years ago." All I could say was, "Better late than never. Most husbands never get it."

Gorillas—In the Wild and in the Home

Studies of male silverback gorillas confirm the incredible power and impact of the male sex drive. The male gorilla is a huge, massively muscled, fierce creature. He strikes fear in the heart of every other animal in the jungle. Except, that is, for the female silverback gorilla. She doesn't seem too impressed.

Researchers have carefully studied the sex habits of gorillas in the wild. Their observations are quite revealing. If the male gorilla has a healthy, regular sex life with his mate, he is a real pussycat. A teddy bear. A big, happy, sweet fur ball. He purrs with contentment and plays with the baby gorillas. He spends time with Mrs. Gorilla, stroking her and goofing off with her in silly gorilla games. He wears a big, peaceful grin on his face.

But if the male silverback is denied sex for three consecutive days, he becomes a very different gorilla. His reaction is not pretty. He whines. He pouts. He begs. He withdraws and sucks his thumb. He cries. He rages. He makes a hooting sound and beats his breast. He's anxious. He's depressed. He bites his nails. He soils himself.

His Number One Need Is Physical Intimacy

I'm not saying that you are married to a male silverback gorilla. Well . . . actually, I am, in the sense that your husband has a very, very strong need to be physical with you on a regular basis.

If you're not regularly making out and having intercourse with your husband, I have some bad news for you: He doesn't feel loved by you.

His need for physical intimacy with you is hardwired into his DNA by God. It is an integral part of his manhood. When this need is not met, he feels like less of a man. He feels unbelievably frustrated. He feels completely rejected by you.

Almost every husband dreams—literally dreams—that some day his wife will be more interested in sex.

I can virtually guarantee that your husband wants more sex, and he especially wants you to be more excited about sex. He wants you to want him physically. There is nothing as invigorating and stimulating to a man as his wife wanting his body.

I have made a shocking breakthrough in my research: Physical affection and sex are important to men. It is a God-given need. That's right, wives. We need sex, and if we don't get it . . . we'll die! Please, save our lives.

Most men really like their wives to be more aggressive in the physical area. Always being the initiator gets old. Very old. Walking down the hall begging and pleading. Tugging at your skirt. "Come to me, please. Touch me. Put your hands on me. Make me feel like a man!"

Women, you know how to do this. Your husband is sitting on the couch watching television or just staring off into space. For once, there are no kids in sight. You go into the bedroom and slip into something more comfortable. You spritz on perfume: *Sensuality under the Palms* or *You Wild Thing*. You glide down the hallway in your slinky outfit, you sit down next to him and cross your legs the way you do, and then all soft and warm and sultry, you say, "Hey, big boy! New in town?"

He won't be able to grab the remote and hit Off fast enough. Even if it's the last twenty seconds of the big game and the score is tied. He'll turn it off without a second thought. You're there, you're looking good, and you want him.

In order for you to pursue him physically in ways like this, I know the two of you must first be *emotionally* connected. I've made that clear. As he steps up and shows progress in emotional intimacy, your job as a wife is to meet his need for *physical* intimacy.

You'll find out along the way that *you* have a deep need for physical intimacy, too! God designed you to enjoy physical passion with your husband. It's time for you to start enjoying it.

I've advised you (and your husband) to take a number of important steps in physical intimacy in the last eleven weeks.

I put some real emphasis on it in Week 5. So hopefully you have already made some progress in touching and connecting physically.

Below are two additional strategies that will help you pursue your husband physically and improve this vital area of your new marriage.

Talk to Him about Sex

It's amazing how many couples never talk to each other about the physical part of their relationship. I mean, never! To them, the subject is awkward, too personal, too risky, too embarrassing. However, it's impossible to develop healthy touch and intercourse if you don't talk about it.

Talk about sex during at least three of your four Couple Talk Times during Week 12. You will go first in each discussion, but hopefully your husband will also share his honest views about your physical relationship.

Discuss the differences between men and women in the area of touch. Tell your partner what is blocking you from really relaxing and enjoying touch. Describe when you want—and don't want—to be touched. What do you like? What do you not like?

Tell the truth. "I would really enjoy it if we . . ." or "I enjoy . . ." Many spouses could have a closet full of Oscars for all the times they've pretended to enjoy sex. And it's not always the woman who is not interested in sex and has to be coaxed into the bedroom. In about 20 to 25 percent of couples, the roles are reversed. The man resists sex, and the woman pursues him. He avoids physical intimacy, and the woman becomes frustrated and continually feels rejected.

There are always reasons for either partner feeling uncomfortable with sex. The only way out is dealing with the issue directly. The resisting partner must ask the Lord for the courage to talk openly and honestly with the spouse about what's going on inside. For many, the prospect of this kind of dialogue is simply unnerving, uncomfortable. And one fear always is that one spouse will be told, or it will be implied, that he or she is inadequate, a poor sex partner. So in these discussions, be careful and gentle and sensitive.

All couples have sexual problems. That's right. I said *all* couples. The only difference is between couples who talk about their sexual problems and couples who do not. The couples who do not discuss sex will never have a deeply intimate, satisfying sex life. The couples who do talk about sex have a good chance—almost 100 percent—to develop and maintain a great sex life.

When you talk about your sexual problems, you can actually discover what is blocking you. You are also being vulnerable, and so, automatically, you reach a deeper level with your partner. With the truth on the table and the two of you connecting on a deeper level, you can work together to resolve your sexual problems. Together is the only way you can resolve them, since sex involves both of you.

Make sure you see any sexual problem as a joint problem, one you both have. It's not: "You've got a problem. Fix it and get back to me." It's not even: "I'll help you with your problem." It needs to be approached as: "*We* have a problem. Let's work on it."

Ninety percent of sexual difficulties can be fixed with open, frank dialogue between the man and the woman. In some cases, the couple will need to see a psychologist or physician to address psychological/medical issues. Because it is a shared problem, always go together. Even if professional help is needed, you will still have to talk in order to work through the problem as a team.

If you don't talk about your physical relationship, nothing can change. Neither partner has any idea how to improve sex. If you talk about it, together you can make significant changes. Talk about it regularly, at least once a month, to keep up-to-date and stay on track.

Schedule Sex with Him

Give up the idea that sex is natural and spontaneous. After the honeymoon, you can kiss that notion good-bye. Let's have a moment of silence for our honeymoon sex. Boy, oh boy, those were the days! Sex was anytime, any place, and more than once a day. No preparation. No obstacles. No problems. Okay, that's enough. Let's get back to the real world.

After the first year of marriage, sex is a whole new ball game. Add a child (or two or three), and suddenly your world is turned upside down. You have even less time, energy, and opportunity for sex. Now you have to prepare. There are obstacles. You both must overcome problems.

If you want to enjoy healthy, regular sex, you have to schedule it.

Wife, I want you to be the one to initiate scheduling sex. Every weekend, on a Saturday or Sunday, sit down with your husband and schedule your sexual times for the upcoming week. This kind of planning has many benefits:

- You'll make sure sex happens even when life is busy.
- Your husband won't be in excruciating limbo, wondering when he can have sex. Also, for the man, anticipation brings him pleasure.
- He won't need to pressure you.
- You won't have to put up with his perhaps crude or clumsy way of asking for sex.
- Both of you will be able to prepare for these special sexual periods.

The Secret to a Successful Marriage

Do you know why 50 percent of all marriages, including Christian marriages, end in divorce? I'll tell you why. It's because husbands and wives are not putting God where he belongs in their marriages. He belongs at the *center*.

When you are doing marriage in your own power, you are doomed to fail. Who are you kidding? Marriage is impossible unless you and your spouse are, on a regular basis, spiritually bonding.

Spiritual bonding is consistently placing God at the very center of your relationship and growing ever closer to him as a couple. Emotional and physical intimacy are critically important needs. But the most important need of all in a marriage is spiritual intimacy.

Spiritual intimacy puts the presence and power of God into your marriage. He is the Source of all love (1 John 4:16), and he will continually energize your love for each other. Your growing spiritual intimacy will bring you as close as a man and woman can get.

You've been doing some quality spiritual bonding in the Change Your Marriage process. You've been reading a couple's devotional and engaging in a period of five minutes of prayer in your Couple Talk Times. You've prayed together as you worked through a number of the assignments in the previous weeks.

I have one particularly effective strategy I want to add to your spiritual bonding equipment.

Talk Spiritually

If you want real depth in your marriage, you need to learn to talk with each other spiritually. When I tell Sandy how God is working in my life, I open a door so she can see inside me. When I share with her how I'm doing in my relationship with Jesus, she really knows me at the core of my being. Because Jesus is the center of my life, I'm sharing the most important part of me.

You learn to tell your partner, regularly and in detail, about your spiritual life: what you're doing in your daily quiet time with God, insights you've gained in your Bible reading, and how you're applying the Bible to your life. You need to talk about your spiritual victories—those times when God gave you the power to share Christ with a coworker, overcome a weakness, or help a friend in need. You also need to admit your spiritual defeats—those times when you failed to obey God, read your Bible regularly, or impact those around you for Christ. When Satan attacks you—and he will—tell your partner and pray about it together.

Each of you can share how God is working in your individual lives and how he is using daily events to guide and teach you. People frequently say to me, "Dave, I just live life, and things happen. I know God is in charge, but he's not really all that involved in the details of my life, is he?" I reply: "Oh yes, if you know him personally through Jesus, he is."

Once you have a relationship with God through Jesus, he is with you twenty-four hours a day. At your request, he's guiding and leading you. "The steps of a man are established by the LORD; and He delights in his way. When he falls, he shall not be hurled headlong; because the LORD is the One who holds his hand" (Ps. 37:23–24 NASB). He's creating events every day to teach you, to develop your character, and to build faith in him. God is choreographing your entire life! Once you open your eyes and see what he's doing, your whole perspective changes. No day is ever again routine, because your sovereign God is the director of every scene, every event, every interaction.

Not only is this attitude toward each day of your life good for your personal spiritual life, but it also provides an inexhaustible supply of conversational material for you and your spouse. You can come home every day and say, "Guess what God did in my life today?"

In fact, God made lots of things happen in your day. All for you! When you start noticing God's involvement in your day, you'll have things to talk about. You'll have some terrific conversations that are personal, revealing, stimulating, and encouraging.

Homework: Week 12

1. Continue to work on improving your relationship with the Lord, stay in contact with your accountability partner, have your four Couple Talk Times per week, go out on one playful date, hold hands, give once-a-day massages, and hug and kiss twice a day. Ask each other: How did I do meeting your needs this week?

2. Husband, use the notepad to prepare for all four of your Couple Talk Times. Also, share your work stress during at least two of your Talk Times.

3. Wife, talk about sex—in the ways mentioned in this chapter—during at least three of your Couple Talk Times. After she shares first, husband, give your input on the sexual topics she has covered.

4. Wife, if you feel ready for intercourse, sit down with your husband on Saturday or Sunday and schedule at least one sexual time for the week.

5. Talk about your individual spiritual lives in two of your Couple Talk Times.

6. If you're ready to begin a personal relationship with God, please go to the appendix in the back of this book for some guidance.

Part 3

The "My Spouse Won't Change" Marriage

14

"I Married a Stick and Now I'm Stuck"

In these chapters, 14 through 16, I refer to the husband as the spouse who won't change. Certainly, it could just as easily be the wife who won't change.

You've read my Change Your Marriage program. You know the steps in the twelve-week change process. I fully understand, and you may, also, that there may be precious little chance your husband will agree to work through the program with you.

Why? Because he's a Stick. *Stick* is my term for a spouse who refuses to change. He wants to stay married to you, but he will do nothing to improve your ailing, unfulfilling, perhaps terminally ill marriage. He has resisted every attempt you've made to change him and your relationship. And he will continue to resist all your attempts at change, because that's what a Stick does.

Profile of a Stick

A Stick is a husband who denies his wife access to his personal, inside life. He locks his intimate thoughts and emotions deep down in an internal vault. He doesn't talk of personal things. He doesn't reveal himself in any way. He doesn't listen well. He doesn't express love.

The Stick is a master at avoiding intimacy and at making you feel guilty for wanting more out of your marriage. He is convinced you have a good marriage. He gets angry when you try to change him.

From all appearances, you are not a priority in his life. The sad truth is, you may not even make his top ten. He has no idea what your real needs are, especially those vital, God-given needs. He's about as romantic as a block of wood. He shows interest in you only when it's for sex. And, of course, the sex is all about him. His orgasm is what it's all about.

Everything is all about him. He has made being selfish into an art form. Chances are good he is or could be a narcissist, a completely self-centered person who thinks only about his own needs and desires. He is unaware of and quite unconcerned about your needs and desires. He truly believes you exist only to serve him and make him happy. If he's happy, then you must be happy. He is the center of the universe.

By definition, the Stick is a lousy husband. He doesn't meet your needs. He won't romance you. He won't make time to be with you. He won't talk to you on a personal level. He won't listen to you when you want to share your thoughts and feelings. He won't be your spiritual leader. He mistreats you. He is emotionally abusive.

If you're getting the impression I believe the Stick is not a good guy, you're right. If your husband is a good guy who loves you, you wouldn't be reading this chapter. (Unless you're reading it to help someone you know who is in a bad marriage.) A genuinely decent husband would agree to join you in following my Change Your Marriage program.

Being Married to a Stick Isn't Pretty

Well, you married a Stick, and now you're stuck. He just won't talk personally, will he? You've tried everything. You've been nice and loving. It doesn't work. You've cried and begged. It doesn't work. You've prayed your heart out. It doesn't work. You've been angry and demanding. It doesn't work. You've given him the silent treatment. It doesn't work. You've threatened him with leaving him, and maybe even with divorce. It doesn't work.

You've dragged him to church and to marriage seminars. You've tried to get him to read marriage books, but a Stick doesn't read. If he does read, he doesn't apply. You've bought CDs and DVDs. You have one of the largest private collections of marriage material in the civilized world. Nothing has worked. Nothing.

Your marriage is dying or already dead. Without an ongoing emotional connection—and you surely don't have that—there can be no real life in a marriage.

He's not meeting your emotional needs. You don't feel understood by him. You don't feel nurtured or cherished by him. You feel disconnected from him. You're angry and resentful and deeply hurt. This is not the marriage you dreamed of having. It's not even close.

He is a boring, life-sucking, stress-causing, and unbelievably frustrating man to live with. You dread living out your life this way.

You get hurt and frustrated and angry each time he fails to love you the way you need to be loved and show you this love in words and actions. But being a good Christian wife, you choke down these painful feelings and soldier on. Maybe tomorrow he'll change. Maybe next week. Maybe this Easter or Christmas. Maybe this coming Valentine's Day. Maybe after he sees two of your closest friends get divorced. Maybe. Maybe. Maybe. But you don't want a divorce.

Each *maybe* that passes adds a little more rejection, a little more disappointment and hurt, a little more anger to the growing pool of resentment in your heart. And any hope disappears. And then you, a good Christian wife, wake up one day and you've had enough. You're through with the maybes. You're through with him. You may have gone five years, seven years, or even twenty years. But you're not going any further.

Your decision to seriously consider exiting the marriage seems terribly sudden. It's not. It's been coming, slowly but surely, for a long time. Your resentments have finally filled your heart, leaving no room for any love for this man. He has robbed you—by one neglect, one hurt, one disappointment, one blasted hope at a time—of realizing your deepest desires for happiness in life.

You don't think this can happen to you? It is *already* happening to you. That's why it's so important to do something about your Stick now, while you still have feelings for him and can respond positively to changes he initiates. If you keep doing what you've been doing, the day will come when you won't have even the incentive to love him anymore. You'll be done and want out of the marriage. You won't care if he changes or not.

You May Not Divorce, but You Will Suffer

Your pain and resentment may not push you into divorce court, and I hope they don't, but they certainly will cause you to suffer in many areas of your life. His mistreatment is killing you slowly.

Your pain will attack your psychological system. You'll be susceptible to a broad range of emotional problems: depression, anxiety, panic attacks, worry, insomnia, lowered self-esteem, an increase in feelings of insecurity, a pattern of negative thinking, cynicism, addiction to food, overspending, alcohol, drugs. . . .

Your pain will travel to the weak areas of your body and wreak havoc. Do you have a history of heart trouble in your family? Then that's where your resentments could go. I've seen resentments cause—or worsen—many physical diseases: kidney problems, back pain, migraines, chronic fatigue syndrome, irritable bowel syndrome, skin conditions, arthritis. . . .

Your relationship with the Lord will also suffer. You desperately need to be close to your heavenly Father. It's your most precious and vital relationship. But your Stick pain will, over time, separate you from God. If you don't forgive your husband (release forgiveness), God won't forgive you (Matt. 6:14–15; 18:21–35; Mark 11:25–26). Plus, tolerating a Stick in such a close, dependent, daily relationship expends so much energy, there is far less to develop your relationship with God.

Your ability to love and nurture and train your children will be severely hampered by your Stick pain. It takes a great deal of emotional and physical energy to interact with children every day. You won't have the necessary energy, because you're spending it to deal with your Stick. You won't have the patience as a mom. You'll be irritable and get angry with your kids often. You'll overreact. You'll yell. You'll punish them too harshly.

You may look to your children for love that you are not receiving from your husband. This is very unhealthy for you and them.

Your Stick's behavior is also killing your marriage. He's not involved in adultery or another flagrant, serious sin (sexual addiction, alcoholism, drug addiction, gambling . . .), but his Stick behavior is just as damaging to your relationship. It is also serious sin. It just takes longer to destroy your love. In the end, the marriage will be just as dead.

Stop kidding yourself. Your Stick doesn't love you. Maybe he hasn't said the words "I don't love you anymore," but his actions and inaction send that message loud and clear.

The truth is, he hasn't loved you for some time. If he ever truly loved you at all. And he's not going to start loving you unless you do something about his disgraceful, hurtful, and sinful behavior.

How about Submission?

Over the past twenty-plus years, I've seen hundreds of women married to Sticks. Most have told me they came to me as a last resort. Most had sought help from a variety of Christian sources: marriage books, pastors, counselors, and friends. They had received the same basic message from these "helpers":

> There isn't much you can do about your situation, honey. The Bible teaches wives to submit to their husbands. If you submit to him and just keep on loving him, he'll eventually change into a godly husband. If he doesn't, well, that's too bad. I guess that's a burden God expects you to bear. Make God your husband. Oh, and keep praying.

This is the same wimpy, walk-all-over-me message that most Christian authorities give to victims of adultery and other flagrant sins! It won't work with big-time sinners, and it won't work with a husband who is mistreating you in other areas.

A number of these wives said they were told by well-meaning advisors to follow the thirty-day "Just love your man" exercise. The idea here is to dedicate yourself for one month to ignoring your husband's intimacy-killing behavior and inattention, and overwhelm him with loving behaviors. Give him affection and sex. Feed him like a king. Fetch his slippers. Rub his back. When he treats you like yesterday's garbage, just smile and carry on. Just be the best little wife in the whole world. At the end of the month, you'll have a brand-new husband. He'll respond to your love with his own love. He'll be so grateful to you for all you've done, he'll change completely.

I've told these women, "That's the dumbest thing I've ever heard. Continuing to love him without expecting anything back is exactly what you've been doing for most of your marriage. It hasn't worked yet, so why would more of the same work now?"

These wives admitted the thirty-day love fest hadn't worked, and they had continued to feel totally unfulfilled and had become even more depressed and discouraged.

Understand the Nature of the Stick

I explained to these wives that the "you must submit and unconditionally love" approach is a complete misunderstanding of the nature and the mind-set of a Stick. Also, it totally disregards the Bible's teaching about the sin nature of man. Furthermore, it fails to help good and loving husbands who, because of ignorance or background or erroneous teaching, are blundering in their treatment of their wives. This husband is blinded by his sin (and Satan) and may not realize he's causing damage to himself, to you, and to the children. Furthermore, very often he believes he's a good guy and has a good marriage. He believes this because you, his wife, are still doing everything for him and have relinquished your rights to love and care and protection. As long as you keep meeting needs and "submitting" to him and his sin, he thinks everything's fine.

If you seem okay with what's happening in the marriage, he's okay with it. He's pretty happy and will even convince himself that you're pretty happy. Sticks can live quite contentedly in marriages with almost zero intimacy and emotional closeness. Wives and husbands who truly love each other "train" each other about what pleases them and what displeases them. Loving wives and husbands respond to this training and more and more fill each other's needs. This does not happen in Stick marriages, and the husbands I'm describing here don't know what they're missing. You do.

You can even tell your husband how unhappy you are, but he won't believe you if you continue to tolerate his sinful behavior and meet his needs. Your words mean nothing to him. He notices and perceives your behavior as acceptance if not approval—of his treatment of you. He doesn't care if you're unhappy—even miserable—as long as you keep on meeting his needs.

Without realizing it, you are enabling him to sin. You are encouraging him to sin. You are part of the problem. As long as you allow him to sin and help him to stay comfortable in his sin, he may do a few nice things for you now and then. He'll toss you a few bones. Just enough to make you think he'll genuinely change. But he won't change! You make his life too easy, so he has no need to change.

God Calls It Sin

"It's time to throw out the bad advice you've been given and take a look at what God says," I tell the wives of Sticks. God says his behavior is sin because it violates his instructions—commands—to all husbands. Your Stick is certainly not loving you "just as Christ loved the church and gave himself up for her" (Eph. 5:25). He is not showing this sacrificial love, loving *as Christ loved the church* and *died* for her. He is not loving you as he loves his own body, as himself (Eph. 5:28–29, repeated in v. 33). He's not leading you as your head *in the same way* as Christ is *his* head (Eph. 5:23). He's not, as Ephesians 5:28–29 commands him, meeting your needs in a very tender, caring manner.

In these passages of Scripture, God defines a husband's love for his wife. Your husband isn't even close to God's definition. He's much closer to the opposite.

In his first epistle, in giving basic instructions to husbands, Peter added a devastating message to husbands who treat their wives poorly: "You husbands in the same way, live with your wives in an understanding way, as with someone weaker, since she is a woman; and show her honor as a fellow heir of the grace of life, so that your prayers may not be hindered" (1 Peter 3:7 NASB).

God wants husbands to understand and do their part in meeting the spiritual, emotional, and physical needs of their wives (some of which only the husband can meet). Husbands are to treat their wives with gentleness, honor, and respect, *treasuring* them and *cherishing* them. Husbands who fail to do so in disobedience of God's commands will be spiritually cut off from God! Their line of communication to God will be disrupted!

This spiritual consequence is the worst thing that could happen to a husband. The withdrawal of fellowship with God is worse than physical, emotional, or career consequences. God takes very seriously a husband's care of his wife, because it is the foundation of a good marriage and of good parenting. God confronts the husband's sin in this area with a decisive and massive strike. So should you.

The Bible Gives You One Option: Confront

Submitting to your husband's sin hurts him. It hurts you. It hurts the kids. It hurts your marriage. And it causes you to sin because you're not following the teaching of the Bible. What do you do with sin? You don't submit to it. You don't enable it. You fight it. You *confront* it (Matt. 5:23–24; 18:15–17). God certainly wants you to confront adultery and all big-time, heinous sins. He also wants you to confront *all other serious sins* in your husband's life.

Stop making excuses for your Stick. Get out of denial and face reality. Many wives of Sticks have told me: "But he had a

bad childhood and has a lot of unresolved personal issues."
I respond: "So what? I agree that he obviously has personal
issues. The only way to motivate him to face his issues and
work on them is to confront his sin and do tough, biblical
love on him. You are likely the only key to this in his life."

Your Stick will change only when he has to. That will be
when he's in pain and crisis. When he knows you will no
longer enable or hide or be silent about his sin. When you
follow the Bible's instructions to expose his sin and hit him
with serious consequences. When he sees he has lost you.

You have no idea the power and influence you can wield
as a wife. Use them! God wants you to use them.

I know a Stick *is* willing to finally address his sin when he
comes into therapy and tells me: "Doc, I think I've lost her."
At first, he'll work just to win her back. Along the way, he'll
genuinely change. He'll own his problem and overcome it for
himself and for God.

The traditional, popular Christian approach to a Stick
doesn't work. *I've never seen it work.* My approach is good
for you and gives you the best chance to change your Stick.
Try it my way.

My way, which I'm convinced is God's way, will empower
you. You will never be the same. You'll be healthier. Stronger.
More assertive. A better parent. A more effective Christian.
No matter what your Stick chooses to do, you'll know you
did *everything* possible to create change in your marriage.
And you'll be ready to move on with your life, if that's how
God directs you.

Homework: Chapter 14

1. How long have you been married to a Stick? When did
   you realize you'd married a Stick? What have you tried
   in your efforts to change him?
2. What has being married to your Stick cost you? Psychologically? Physically? Spiritually? As a parent? How

much longer are you willing to accept this and suffer the consequences?

3. What advice have you received from others (pastors, family members, friends, best-selling books) regarding how to deal with your Stick? Have you been told to submit? By "submit" I do not mean willingly wanting and following your husband's leadership, but instead, accepting behavior that is the opposite of what God commands husbands. Have you been told to just keep loving him, and he'll change?

4. Are you ready to accept that your Stick is in serious sin and that you are enabling his sin?

5. Are you ready to obey the Bible and confront him?

15

Your Stick's Last Chance

Are you sick and tired of being mistreated by your husband? Are you weary of feeling depressed and devastated by his ongoing rejection of you? Are you through taking his abuse? Have you finally had it with his refusal to love you and be the kind of husband you want and need? If you answered yes to these questions, it's time to get to work. It's time to go to war.

That's right. This is going to be a war. You're fighting for yourself, your children, and your marriage. This will be your Stick's last chance to win you back and change his marriage. The old marriage is over. Finished. You're not going back to it. With or without him, you're moving on.

Your message to your Stick is: "We build a new marriage or bust."

Before we get into my Battle Plan, I want you to understand one thing. You are now operating independently of your husband's authority and leadership. His serious sin has disqualified him from his position of headship. As I hope I made clear in the previous chapter, you are not to submit to sin. You are not to encourage and support it in any way. You are to go to war with it and with the person who's committing it.

You will not ask your husband's permission to take the specific steps in my Battle Plan. Good thing, because it's likely he'll hate what you're doing and fight you tooth and nail. He'll be desperate to stop you because he wants to protect and nurture his sin. He wants to guard his flawed view of himself and his reputation. His angry, defensive reaction will just confirm that you're on the right track.

My Battle Plan will give you the best chance to bring real change and intimacy to your loveless marriage. I firmly believe it's what God wants you to do.

The Foundation: Matthew 18:15–17

The foundation of my Battle Plan is Matthew 18:15–17. These verses teach a wife how to confront her husband:

> If your brother sins, go and show him his fault in private; if he listens to you, you have won your brother. But if he does not listen to you, take one or two more with you, so that "by the mouth of two or three witnesses every fact may be confirmed." If he refuses to listen to them, tell it to the church; and if he refuses to listen even to the church, let him be to you as a Gentile and a tax collector.
>
> NASB

My focus in this chapter is the first confrontation mentioned in this passage: the one-on-one confrontation between you and your husband. You will take a series of action steps in this first level of confrontation.

If your Stick resists your one-on-one confrontational efforts and refuses to work on the marriage, then you will immediately move through the final three confrontations taught in this Matthew 18 passage: "take one or two more with you," "tell it to the church," and "let him be to you as a Gentile and a tax collector." Chapter 16 describes these three final confrontations.

Battle Step 1: Stay Close to God

This step almost goes without saying, but I'll say it anyway. You are going into spiritual warfare against Satan and what your husband is doing. So you must have the Lord by your side every inch of the way. Never forget that, when dealing with sin and the enemy of our souls, you are fighting not flesh and blood but "spiritual forces of wickedness" (Eph. 6:12 NASB), and you will need to put on "the full armor of God" (Eph. 6:11,13). You will need to be "strong in the *Lord*" (Eph. 6:10, emphasis added). Since you are on his side, the battle and the outcome are not yours; they are the Lord's, as David proclaimed before he killed the giant Goliath (1 Sam. 17:47). The Lord will fight with you, for you, and through you *if* you are closely connected to him.

Battle Step 2: Sign Up a Support Team

No one goes into a major battle alone. If you do, you won't have a chance. I hope you already have the accountability partner I mentioned in Chapter 2. But one person isn't enough for your support team.

Carefully select a small group—a platoon—of family members and friends who will go into battle with you. At least two of these fellow soldiers should live in your local area. When choosing supporters, find people you know have shown forgiveness for others in the past or had their own marital struggles and are open about them, and are not rigid in their views. The reason for this is to help you all move on once your marriage is unstuck. Supporters sometimes have more difficulty forgiving and forgetting the actions of your spouse than you do. In fact, before you tell a potential supporter what happened, I suggest asking them if they will be

192

able to forgive and move on once you say the recovery has taken place. Keep in mind even when you've chosen carefully, it is possible some of your supporters will not remain close friends after this process. Your marriage has to be more important than the friendship.

Gather your platoon members, and tell them the entire truth about your husband's sinful behavior, your role in enabling it, the ways it has affected you, and just how bad your marriage is.

Tell your Support Team about my book and the Matthew 18:15–17 approach you intend to follow. Ask your supporters to read Chapters 1 through 16 of this book so they fully understand and agree with the action steps you're going to take. Read Matthew 18:15–17 out loud and pray together that God will use these steps to break your husband and cause him to genuinely confess and repent and work toward restoration.

Ask for regular prayer. And pray regularly with your small group of trusted supporters. In addition to spiritual support, ask for emotional support, and even financial support if needed. Ask these faithful warriors to push you to be strong and to press the attack against your husband's sin. Ask them to be there whenever you need them. Be sure to keep them apprised of how things are going in answer to their prayers.

Battle Step 3: See a Therapist If Necessary

Sometimes, wives I see in therapy are not ready to follow the Stick Battle Plan. Because of past unresolved issues and an entrenched pattern of codependent, passive behavior, they are paralyzed with fear. They are simply not healthy enough to do battle with their Sticks . . . yet.

You may be in this category. If you are, that's okay. It's nothing to be ashamed about. It just means you will need some extra help before you continue with the Battle Plan.

To find out if you're strong enough yet, read the rest of this chapter and Chapter 16. If after reading my Battle Steps you decide you're not ready to follow my tough-love approach, find a Christian therapist who can help you get ready.

You will be looking for two things from your therapy. First, insight into why you have tolerated your husband's sin. What are the reasons you have been unable to stand up to your husband and demand change? Is it because of how you were raised? Does it go back to a distant, uncaring, rejecting father? Is it abuse you suffered as a child? Is it a transfer of unresolved pain and guilt from an abortion, premarital sex, or some other secret sin? Is it a lack of full recovery from a divorce? Is it poor self-esteem or a passive, compliant personality? Is it the incorrect teaching of your church on submission?

With God's guidance and a good Christian therapist, you can find out what it is that is causing you to be an enabler and a victim of your spouse's neglect and/or sin. It may be one or more of these possibilities I've listed. When you discover why you enable, you'll be able to do the work that will make you an emotionally healthy, assertive wife. A wife who will draw a line in the sand and say, "This far and no further." A wife who will stop her part in the sinful marital pattern, will force her husband to be all alone in his sin, and help him find his way to spiritual and emotional health.

The second thing you want from your therapy—from your therapist—is a tough, take-no-prisoners approach. Don't waste your time and money with a therapist who recommends a weak, wimpy "just love him and pray a lot" strategy. You need a therapist who will agree with my basic Battle Plan.

You want a therapist who will train you for war and guide you through it.

When you've done your individual work in therapy, return to my Battle Plan, and pick up at Battle Step Four.

Battle Step 4: Get Ready Financially

When you confront your husband and stop playing your part in the sin, the situation could get ugly. It's very common for a sinning husband to retaliate by squeezing his wife financially. If he can swing it, you'd better expect him to cut off the money as a way of punishing you, shutting you up, and trying to get you back into the codependent role.

Do what you have to do to make sure you'll have money for you and the children. Ask family members, friends, and church leaders to be ready to help you with money. (Don't expect help from those who think you should tolerate—in the name of "submission" or whatever—his mistreatment and do nothing about it.)

Get a job, if necessary. Get your own bank account with your name only on it. It would be wise to consult an attorney to find out how much money you can legally take—if you need to—from checking, savings, and investment accounts. Also, arrange a place to stay if you and the kids need to leave the home temporarily. However, do this only if your attorney advises it. It is essential that you maintain rights to the house.

Battle Step 5: The First Confrontation

Go to your husband, ask him to sit down, look into his eyes, and in the most serious tone you can muster, say these words:

(His Name), there's something very important I want to talk to you about. It concerns the future of our marriage. I'm not ready to take this step now. I'm still sorting through some things. I want the kids out of the house when we talk. It needs to be just the two of us. Let's meet and do this in three days, on *(day of the week)*.

After you have scheduled the meeting, stand up and go about your business. He may ask you what this is all about. Don't tell him anything. He has to wait until the meeting. Spend the next three days being cool, reserved, and pulled back from him. Nothing dramatic. You're just in a quiet, contemplative mood. A little mystery is a good thing for a man. You want him to wonder, even worry, about what you are going to say. You want this meeting to have a real impact on his life.

If he's a bona fide dirtball, he won't care at all. He may even smirk or laugh at you. But if there is anything good left in him, he *might* just feel pressure and fear and guilt. Let's hope and pray that will be so.

READ YOUR CONFRONTATION LETTER

At the appointed time and place (probably in your home), sit down with your Stick and confront him with his mistreatment of you. Have everything you are going to say written down. It's easy to forget what you intend to say in the intensity and awkwardness of the situation. Plus, after the meeting, you'll hand him a copy of what you read.

Ask him to be silent until you have finished reading your statement. If he keeps interrupting you, hand the letter to him and walk away. If he refuses to listen to you, just hand the letter to him and walk away. If he gets belligerent and hostile, hand the letter to him and walk away. You're not going to listen to even one more rationalization, defensive comment, or sarcastic barb. After you have read the letter, hand the letter to him and walk away.

You won't listen to anything he may want to say at this meeting. Talk—at least, with him—is cheap, and usually painful. All you're interested in is action.

Be brief and to the point. This meeting should not take more than five minutes. Don't show much emotion as you read your message. Being cool, calm, and collected will make him realize you mean business. This is either the beginning of the end of this marriage or the beginning of the creation of a good marriage. It is just that momentous. Your job is to make him believe he has, as of now, irrevocably lost you. You are through with the old marriage. This will be his last chance to win you back.

I've included a sample Letter of Confrontation delivered by one wife to her Stick. Feel free to use the same format when you confront your husband.

(His Name),

I'm tired of our lousy marriage. I'm tired of trying to get you to change, to open up and talk to me, to meet my needs, to love me the way I long to and need to be loved. *I've tolerated a lot of pain and mistreatment from you, and that's my fault. I've tried way too hard in this marriage, and you haven't tried hardly at all.*

I'm through with our old marriage. I will never go back to it. I'm done. I will not sacrifice my health and the well-being of our kids any longer. I'm moving on—with or without you.

Maybe I'm crazy, but I've got one more try left in me. When I say one, I mean one. It's only because of God, the kids, and my conscience that I'm giving you one final chance to win me back and build a new, good, happy marriage. Frankly, I don't care either way. It's up to you.

I've decided to do Dr. David Clarke's 90-Day Change Your Marriage Program. You can join me in doing it if you want to. I'm starting Dr. Clarke's program one week from now. If you choose to join me, read Chapters 1 through 13 in his book— you have seen me reading it—in the next seven days and let me know you're ready to start.

If you choose not to, that's fine. I'll do it myself so I can be a healthier person as I begin my new life. If, at any point after deciding not to do this with me, you change your mind and want to do the program with me, let me know. We'll go back to the beginning, and I'll start over with you.

(Your Name)

Hand him your letter and my book, and walk away with no discussion whatsoever. Don't bring up the subject again. Don't ask him if he's read the chapters. Don't ask him if he will join you in the Twelve-Week process. Say nothing at all about it to him. If he says nothing about it, which is a very high possibility, simply begin my program in one week.

If You Have to Go It Alone

If you do my program alone, you won't be going the full twelve weeks. It makes no sense to do certain steps in my Marriage Recovery Plan when you have a husband who refuses to even try to improve the relationship. As the Bible states in Matthew 7:6, "Do not throw your pearls before swine" (NASB).

Most of my clients who do my program alone take about six weeks to finish it.

At the beginning of each action step you complete, you will tell him what you're going to do and ask him to join you in the Change process by following that step. If he says no, you'll do the assignment and then share with him what you've done. When you tell him about the assignment you did, make it very brief and do not ask for a response. Tell him, and walk away.

If at any point in the process your husband tells you he does want to join you in the Twelve-Week Plan, schedule another one-on-one meeting. At this meeting, he needs to convince you he's serious about doing the work necessary, no matter how he might dislike parts or how painful they might be, to improve your marriage.

If you like his attitude and believe he is sincere, ask him to read Chapters 1 through 13 in one week. When he's finished reading, you'll start the Twelve Weeks together.

Also, at this meeting, tell your husband that he may need some individual therapy with a licensed, Christian therapist before he can successfully complete the Twelve Weeks. He

198

is a Stick because of unresolved pain and learned dysfunction from past relationships with family members. His self-centeredness and unwillingness even to try to emotionally connect with you are barriers he erects to protect himself from being hurt again. His behavior may be—to him—a way to survive, harmful as it is. It has been all that he has known. It seems to him to have worked. Comprehending this and believing there is a better way for him and your marriage could make all the difference.

If you both realize—whether before or during the twelve weeks—he needs some therapy, he needs to get some therapy. Knowing how little he has ever opened up to you suggests the considerable value of his talking to a professional who can help him. You will be involved in his therapy and be supportive (state this strongly to him) as he works through his issues. When he's healthy enough, the two of you will start the Twelve Weeks together.

Battle Step 6: Tell Him, Do It, Move On

Okay, your Stick has refused to do my Twelve Weeks with you. No huge surprise there. So you're ready to do it alone. Here's what I want you to do.

WEEK 1: REBUILD FROM THE GROUND UP

At the beginning of Week 1, tell your husband you'll be working to get closer to God with a daily time with him and with regular church attendance. Tell him you will find an accountability partner who will support you through the Change Your Marriage steps. Tell him Dr. Clarke also recommends that couples establish four twenty-to-thirty-minute Couple Talk Times per week. Let him know that, unless he chooses to work with you in this Change program, there's no point in having these Couple Talk Times.

Ask him if he will join you in this Change Your Marriage process.

At the end of Week 1, briefly tell him what you've done to begin strengthening your relationship with God and cultivating your fellowship with him. Also, tell him who your accountability partner is.

Weeks 2 and 3: "I'm Wrong, I'm Sorry, I'll Change"

Tell him you'll be writing a Letter of Responsibility to him, and mention the four areas it will contain: confessing your sins, feelings of sorrow, asking for forgiveness, and changing your behavior. Tell him you will read this Letter to him at the end of the week. Tell him you'll come up with your Top Two mistakes from your Letter (decide on your own what your Top Two will be; don't ask him for input). And tell him you will work to correct these mistakes during Week 3.

Ask him if he will join you in this Change Your Marriage process.

Read your Letter of Responsibility to him. If he refuses to listen, take your Letter and walk away. Don't hand the Letter to him. If he chooses to listen, read your Letter, and after reading it, hand it to him and walk away. Don't ask for any response. Take a week and work on correcting your Top Two. You'll work on your Top Two for this one week only.

Weeks 4 and 5: Pump In the Positives

Describe for him, briefly, the positive and romantic behaviors Dr. Clarke recommends for Weeks 4 and 5. Tell him that, because of his lack of interest in improving your marriage, you won't be doing any of these behaviors. Nor will you be asking him to do any. Tell him if he wants to know more about these positive and romantic behaviors, he can read those chapters in Dr. Clarke's book.

Ask him if he will join you in this Change Your Marriage process.

WEEK 6: LEARN HOW TO FIGHT

Tell him you have learned a better, more effective way to resolve conflicts. Tell him that, since the two of you are not working together to improve your marriage, it makes no sense for you to explain to him Dr. Clarke's Conflict Resolution formula. If he wants to know what the formula is, he can read that chapter.

Ask him if he will join you in this Change Your Marriage process.

WEEKS 7 AND 8: HEAL FROM YOUR PAST PAIN

Tell him you'll be writing Past Pain Transfer Letters and, very briefly, describe the purpose of these Letters: to clean out pain from your past and eliminate its harmful transfer to your marriage. Tell him you'll read these letters to him at the end of the week. Don't mention the Follow-Up Talks, because there is no point in having them with a spouse who isn't working on the marriage.

Ask him if he will join you in this Change Your Marriage process.

Read your Past Pain Transfer Letters to him. If he refuses to listen, take your Letters and walk away. Don't hand the Letters to him. If he chooses to listen, read your Letters and walk away. Don't ask for any response.

WEEKS 9 AND 10: FORGIVE EACH OTHER

Tell him you'll be writing a Letter of Forgiveness to him. Tell him you will be cleaning out all your resentments against him and forgiving him completely. Tell him this will be Release Forgiveness and not Intimacy Forgiveness (these are explained in the book if he wants to know more), because he is choosing not to reconcile or even work toward it in the kind of program you are following. Tell him you'll read this letter to him at the end of the week. Don't mention the Follow-Up Talks, because there won't be any.

Ask him if he will join you in this Change Your Marriage process.

Read your Letter of Forgiveness to him. If he refuses to listen, take your letter and walk away. Don't hand it to him. If he chooses to listen, read your letter and walk away. Don't ask for or regard any response.

WEEKS 11 AND 12: MEET YOUR DEEPEST NEEDS

Tell him, briefly, that Dr. Clarke spends two chapters on meeting needs in marriage. Tell him you believe one of the reasons your marriage has failed is because real needs have not been met. Tell him you'd be willing to work on meeting his needs if he's willing to work on improving your marriage. Tell him if he wants to know more about needs, he can read those chapters in the book.

Ask him—one last time—if he will join you in this Change Your Marriage process.

You've Done All You Can Do

You have, in these six weeks or so of following my Change plan alone, given your husband every possible opportunity to choose to work on your marriage. He has deliberately rejected every opportunity.

It's painfully clear he doesn't love you. Not even a little bit. Not even enough to try a program designed to make his marriage better. The only person he loves is himself. He has no intention of winning you back and saving his marriage. He couldn't care less about you, the children, and the marriage.

He's taken his stand. Now, it's time for you to bring out the really heavy artillery in this war.

Homework: Chapter 15

1. Follow through on Battle Steps 1 through 4:
   - Stay close to God
   - Sign up a support team
   - See a therapist if necessary
   - Get ready financially
2. Schedule the First Confrontation and read your Confrontation Letter.
3. Move through my Twelve-Week program alone, following my guidelines for each step.
4. If at any point in the process your husband says he wants to join you in the Twelve-Week Plan, have a meeting in which he has to convince you that he's serious about change. If his attitude and commitment are acceptable, ask him to read Chapters 1 through 13, and then you will start the Twelve Weeks together.

16

Rock Your Stick's World

Going through the Change Your Marriage program alone has made you a healthier and stronger person. You're closer to God. You have an improved sense of your worth, especially in God's sight. You have a Support Team in place. You may have received guidance from a therapist. You've taken action to protect yourself financially.

You've identified your main mistakes in the marriage and have worked to correct them. You've understood the importance of positive and romantic behaviors in a marriage. You've learned how to resolve conflicts, a basic, essential tool in a good marriage. You've healed from the pain in your past and eliminated the transfer of that pain to your marriage.

You can clearly see all of your Stick's mistreatment and why you have tolerated it. You have forgiven him for all the hurtful things he's done in your relationship. You have realized the critical role needs play in a marriage.

He's an Industrial-Strength Stick

Something else—something very important—has happened to you as a result of doing the Change Your Marriage program alone. Your resolve to stop putting up with your husband's sinful, harmful behavior is stronger. Much stronger. Over the past six weeks, he has repeatedly refused your offers to join you in the Change Your Marriage program.

Your Stick had his chances, and he blew them all. Just as he's blown thousands and thousands of chances over the years. The difference now is that he will finally face the consequences. The consequences God wants him to face, for God loves him and waits for him to come to him.

He has confirmed his status as an industrial-strength, world-class Stick. He does not love you and has no intention of making any changes. You're fed up, and you ought to be. You're angry, and you ought to be.

You're ready for the final three confrontations of Matthew 18:15–17, and you ought to be.

I want you to move immediately to these three other steps of confrontation. No final speeches. No lectures. No impassioned pleas. No "I can't believe you won't try." No "You have broken my heart." Don't waste your breath. Simply do what the Bible tells you to do.

Gather your Support Team again and inform them that your husband did not respond to the first confrontation (Matt. 18:15). Tell them you're ready to do the final three confrontations. Pray together that God will use these confrontations to break your husband and change his sinful heart. Ask your team to be praying during each of the coming confrontations.

"Take One or Two More with You"

Quickly gather one or two of your closest friends, family members, or other supporters and go with them to confront your husband. Do not stall. Move with speed. The clear sense of Matthew 18 is to take these steps quickly, one right after the other. You have waited long enough for the man to change.

Do not give your husband any warning. This is a surprise attack. Just show up.

One of these "witnesses" should be a man who knows your husband well. Let this man do the talking. He gives this message to your husband: "You are sinning. You need to repent and take action to genuinely change as a husband. You have one week to show your wife and us that you're serious about changing. If you choose to not take the right steps to win your wife back, you will face serious consequences."

Don't tell him what the consequences will be. Let him wonder.

"Tell It to the Church"

If he is unmoved after seven days, go immediately to your pastor and the leaders of your church. Take your "witnesses" with you. Explain in detail the pitiful state of your marriage, the steps you've taken to try to change it, and how your husband is sinning against you and God. Tell these leaders you have already moved through the first two confrontations required by Matthew 18. Urge them to form a team and to go quickly to your husband and do an intervention.

Don't be shocked if your church leaders fail to follow through and deal with your husband. Many pastors and leadership board members will not agree with the assertive, tough-love action you're taking. They'll ask you to be patient and submissive. They'll tell you that if you just love him enough, he'll change. They may even blame you for your marriage problems.

Don't hold your breath, waiting for them to confront your husband. In addition to not agreeing with my approach, they may not have the guts to confront. Confrontation is tough, and many church leaders avoid doing it. Some church leaders will confront sinners and exercise church discipline, but most won't. Refusing to confront your husband certainly means they will not bring this before the church (Matthew 18:17a), either. If your leaders haven't done the intervention in three weeks, move on to the next step in God's plan.

"Let Him Be to You as a Gentile and a Tax Collector"

Your husband has weathered three interventions—or two, if your pastor and his team have choked and done nothing—and isn't about to budge from his sin. Your job now is to shake him as he's never been shaken before in his life. You're at the end of the Matthew 18 process and will immediately and without discussion "let him be to you as a Gentile and a tax collector." You won't divorce him. I never recommend divorce. You will at first shun him. Shunning a serious sinner is also taught in 1 Corinthians 5:9–11. If that doesn't break him, you'll physically separate from him, being certain that you are protected legally and that this will not jeopardize your rights.

Tell Your Children the Truth

Just before you begin shunning, call a private meeting with your children who live in the home. You'll telephone and talk with those who no longer live at home full-time. Your husband is not invited to or welcome at this meeting.

Tell your children exactly what you're doing and why. Tell them Daddy is sinning by treating you badly. Give them appropriate, specific examples of his mistreatment. Explain what you've done to try to get him to change. Read the Matthew 18 passage and describe the interventions you've done to obey God's Word.

Tell your children about my book and the six weeks you just spent—alone—working through the Change Your Marriage program. Tell them how he refused all your offers to join you in the program. Tell them about the second and third Matthew 18 confrontations.

Let them know that you'll be shunning Dad in an attempt to force true repentance. Be clear that if Dad doesn't respond to the shunning, you'll be taking steps to separate from him. Pray with them that Dad will repent and decide to change.

Your children need to know why suddenly you will be ignoring their father. If you don't give them at least a general explanation, they'll be confused and could potentially blame you for being so hard on Dad.

You are not mean or vicious or hateful in how you talk about their father. You simply tell the truth about his sinful behavior and the biblical steps you are taking in response to it.

You do not ask your children to also shun Dad. You will allow and even encourage them to continue to have a relationship with him. You actually want them to express to Dad their feelings about what's happening and to ask him about his mistreatment of you.

Sometimes an older child—after prayer and thorough discussion with you and possibly with a Christian therapist—will choose to shun Dad. If a child makes the choice to shun, you'll support that decision.

You need to know that just being told of the marital problems and then watching you shun their father will stress your kids to the max. Your honesty with them will help reduce their level of insecurity and pain. Realizing Mom and Dad are very unhappy and not being told anything about it is terrifying to children. Usually, the picture that children create is far worse than the actual situation. But the whole ongoing situation is still very traumatic for them.

Knowing what's going on provides the best protection you can give your children. Knowing what's going on helps them begin their adjustment to a possible separation and/or divorce. We don't want a separation or a divorce; that is the reason for my marital recovery program. But if your husband continues on his sinful path, it could happen. It's better for your kids to start dealing with this possibility now than to cruise ignorantly along and suddenly be told your marriage is in terrible shape and you have to separate. This trauma is far worse than the trauma created by telling them up front what is going on.

Plus, the pained reaction of your children to your shunning may help break your husband. As he sees their shock and anguish, maybe he'll realize what he's doing. As he attempts to answer their questions about what's going on, maybe he'll realize what he's doing. What he's putting your kids through now is merely a short preview of what they'll endure if a divorce ensues. Maybe that truth will dawn on him. Even if it doesn't, you and the kids will have begun the torturous path of adjusting to life without him in the home.

Seriously consider going with your children to a Christian family therapist. If you are seeing a therapist and that therapist has experience working with children, you could continue with him or her. Your kids need to express their pain, deal openly with the trauma and tremendous loss Dad is causing, and begin adjusting to the possibility of life without him in the home.

Shun Him

After you talk with the children, take your wedding ring off and shun your husband for one full month.

Shunning means you go as far as you can in an attempt to act as though he doesn't exist. You bring communication down to the lowest level possible. Excluding money issues, the children's schedule, and health emergencies, unless you absolutely have to, say nothing to him. Nothing at all. No "Hello." No "Good morning." No "How was your day?" When he talks to you, ignore him. When he asks you questions, don't answer them.

Like an idiot, he'll probably ask you, "Why are you doing this?" Say nothing. He knows exactly why you're doing it. He'd love to get you into an argument. But the time for arguing and fighting with him is over. He wants to know he can still get a rise out of you because that will mean he still has room to maneuver and manipulate. You want him to believe that you're over him. That, as things stand now, you don't care anymore. That you are not in the slightest bit interested in the man he has chosen to become. That nothing he can say means a thing to you; all that would mean anything to you is for him to repent. When you must say something to him, be as brief and businesslike and cold as you can possibly be.

I want you to stop all services for your husband. No sex. Period. Not even any physical affection of any kind. He has lost, for at least one month, the sacred privilege of coming near you physically. Don't sleep in the same bed with him during the shunning period. Without a word, move his pillow and a sheet and blankets to a guest room or the living room. If there's another bathroom in the house he can use, move all of his toiletries in there. If you have another room he can live in, move all of his clothes in there.

If he moves all of his stuff back into your bedroom and bathroom and refuses to move, then you move to the other bedroom and bathroom. It ought to give you the creeps to be in the same bed with him, to be in the same bedroom with him, and to share the same bathroom with him. So don't do it.

Don't do any laundry for him. Don't iron any clothes for him. Don't buy anything for him. Don't run any errands for him. Don't set a place for him at the table. Don't prepare any food for him. Make meals for you and the children. He's on his own and can forage for himself at mealtimes. If he sits down at the table and takes food, let him eat. Just ignore him.

During this month of shunning, avoid all social contact with him. No dates. No talks of any kind. Don't sit with him at church or any school functions if these meetings fall in the one month period. Don't drive in the car with him. Don't spend any family time with him and the kids. Don't go on any vacations with him. You're not a happy family, thanks to him, so don't pretend.

You're giving him a taste of life without you, which he has set up because of his mistreatment of you. You're giving him—actually, ramming down his throat—a taste of divorce. Will he like it? You'll find out over the next month.

Separate from Him

If, after this month of shunning, he still stubbornly refuses to change, make your preparations to physically separate. As I mentioned in the previous chapter, see a reputable Christian attorney (without your husband's knowledge) to determine your rights and what monies you are entitled to in a separation.

It's sad, and scary, that it has come to this. But separation—in my opinion—is taught in Matthew 18:15–17. This brutal, in-your-face passage ends with the sinner being removed from the local body of Christ. I believe there is clear application to the marriage relationship. There are no qualifiers in this passage of Scripture. No exceptions are made for spouses. You, his spouse, are in the local body of Christ. So you, too, are to remove him from your presence. That means from your home.

Obviously, separation may take some time. Tell your children what you're doing and why. Break your silence with your husband by asking him to leave the home. If he refuses or is obviously stalling, move out with the children (with your attorney's advice). If you can't afford to move out or have no place to go, remain at home and stay in the shunning mode.

If you do separate physically, the separation needs to be a complete separation. It needs to be a "Hell hath no fury like a woman scorned" separation. Have no contact with him except to cope with emergencies, to discuss money, and to deal with the children. No friendly chats, in person or on the telephone. These little fireside chats would serve to ease his guilty conscience and remove all the impact of the separation. You don't want to make him comfortable. You want to make him miserable. You want him to fully comprehend that this is the beginning of the end unless he chooses to stop it.

You have nothing to say to him. You are as cold and unmoving as a glacier. The only talking you'll do is to his friends and family. Of course, you will inform both families and your friends about his sin and the separation. Tell all those people about his mistreatment of you and his refusal to rebuild the marriage. If they want to try to talk some sense into him, fine.

He'll want to come in the house when he just "drops by" or is picking up the kids. Don't let him in. Set up a strict visitation schedule he will follow to see the children. Use the exact schedule that a court would order in a divorce. Ask an attorney what this schedule would be. When he comes to get the kids, let him honk the horn or stand and wait on the porch. You'll send the kids out to him and shut the door behind them. When he brings them back, say nothing, and don't look at him. Just shuffle the kids back inside.

Just as when you were shunning him, include him in no family times. Don't sit with him in church or at school functions and sports events. Don't invite him to the kids' birthday celebrations. He can set up his own birthday parties for them. Don't get together with him for Easter, Thanksgiving, Christmas, New Year's Day, Groundhog Day, or any other holiday.

Don't ask for his help for anything. Don't let him mow your lawn. Don't ask him to clean the pool. Don't let him fix the appliances or do any home repairs. Don't let him take care of your car. If you allow him to do any of these things, that's not a separation. That's not what happens after a divorce. You don't want him to feel like a good, magnanimous, helping guy. You want him to feel like a pariah. A wretched, lost

212

soul who's on the outside—of your and your children's love and respect—looking in. Ask family, friends, neighbors, and church members to help you repair things, or hire a repair person.

This complete separation sends your husband the best message you can send him: "I will not tolerate your mistreatment any longer. Here's what life is like without me. You've lost me. It's over." You're giving him a full taste of divorce. Make him believe you are through with him and your marriage, and you're moving on to better things.

"What If He Wants to Work on the Marriage?"

If at any point in the final three confrontations process he shows signs of breaking and wanting to repent, be wary and stay pulled back. Do not jump back into his arms. Talk and promises are cheap. You require specific actions. If you're separated, stay separated. If he says he's ready to change, hand him a list of what he needs to do:

1. He will see a Christian psychologist or therapist of *your* choosing.
2. You both will go to the first session so you can give the counselor the true picture. Your husband will go through at least two months of individual therapy and work on his personal issues and blocks to intimacy. He'll sign a release so you can get regular updates from the therapist.
3. He'll work with this Christian counselor to find out why he has treated you so badly and why he stubbornly refused to join you in the Change Your Marriage program. He'll take a penetrating look at his family, unresolved pain and traumas in the past, and his weaknesses as a person, husband, and father. Over a two-month period, he will see the counselor at least eight times.

213

4. He'll meet with your pastor (you'll both be at the first meeting), and they'll develop a spiritual growth program he'll follow for two months. It will include regular church attendance, a small group Bible study, a men's support group like Promise Keepers or Men's Fraternity, and one-on-one discipleship. He'll continue the support group and discipleship relationship for at least one full year.

5. He'll find a godly man who will serve as his accountability partner. This could be the same guy who is discipling him. They'll meet face-to-face once a week. He will have an accountability partner for the rest of his life.

6. He will agree to follow the Twelve-Week Change Your Marriage program. He'll read Chapters 1 through 13 and let you know when he's ready to begin.

If he follows through on these behaviors and shows a good attitude and real progress after two months, only then will you begin to respond favorably to him. You will agree to do my Twelve Weeks with him. If he falls back into his selfish and sinful ways, you will immediately go back to shunning and separation.

The Road Ahead

If he chooses not to change, you'll forgive him and keep on forgiving him. That's what the Bible teaches you to do (Matt. 18:21–22; Col. 3:13). God doesn't want bitterness to destroy you. But you won't reconcile. You'll keep your heart, mind, and body away from him until he repents.

If he chooses not to change, you have your answer. He doesn't want you or the marriage, and he'll continue to be involved in serious, ongoing sin. As I have already stated, I never recommend divorce. That is for God to decide. Stay in shunning and separation mode and pray for God's guidance. God will reveal what he wants you to do.

I hope and pray you don't have to carry out these final three Matthew 18 confrontations. But you may have to do it. Don't hesitate. Gather your Support Team, and with Jesus at your side, do it.

Homework: Chapter 16

1. Confront your husband with one or two of your Support Team members. One of these "witnesses" should be a man who knows your husband well.
2. Go to your pastor and the leaders of your church and, with your "witnesses" with you, ask them to confront your husband. Allow them three weeks to act.
3. After telling your children what you are doing and why, shun your husband for one full month.
4. When these confrontations fail, if you are able to, separate from your husband. Make it as complete a separation as possible.
5. If at any point in these final confrontations your husband shows signs of wanting to change and work on the marriage, hand him the six-item list. If he shows real progress on the list's behaviors after two months, ask him to join you in doing my Twelve-Week program.

Part 4

The "My Spouse Has Sinned Big Time" Marriage

17

Make Your Spouse's Serious Sin the Only Issue

These next three chapters, 17 through 19, are intended for couples in which one spouse has committed a serious* sin during the marriage: adultery, pornography, alcoholism, drug addiction, gambling, verbal abuse, physical abuse, workaholism, or reckless financial irresponsibility. Although it wouldn't be a bad idea to read these chapters so you can help others in this situation, if this is not the case in your marriage, you can skip ahead to Chapter 20.

The Week 1 foundational steps will prove very helpful to you both as you heal from the damage caused by the serious sin. Your *Spiritual Growth* will give you God's strength. Your *Accountability Partners* will be an invaluable source of support. Your regular *Couple Talk Times* will provide a forum for many talks about the sin and its traumatic impact.

---

* I fully realize that all sins are serious. However, there are sins that, if not dealt with, will utterly devastate a spouse and destroy a marriage.

Dealing with a spouse's serious sin will take at least two to three months if all goes well. It's likely you'll need to ask a Christian therapist or your pastor to guide you through the recovery steps. Obviously, this serious sin healing process will extend the time required for my Change Your Marriage program. When your healing from the serious sin—as individuals and as a couple—is well on its way, you will return to my 90-day program and do Weeks 2 and 3.

In Chapters 17 through 19, I identify the husband as the sinning spouse. The only reason for this is to avoid the awkward switching back and forth between the masculine and feminine pronouns, he or she, him or her. The wife could be the sinning spouse.

Why Isn't the Sinning Spouse Blamed?

A married couple came to see me for the first time. I'll call them Bob and Susie. Susie, in tears, told me Bob had committed a serious, damaging sin, and they wanted to deal with it as a couple.

Before seeing me, they had sought advice from their pastor, a Christian therapist, several best-selling Christian books, and some close friends. They got the same four pieces of advice from every one of these Christian sources, and all the advice was directed at Susie.

Susie Was Told Bob's Sin Was Partly Her Fault

She wasn't meeting all of Bob's needs. Bob wasn't happy at home. Men don't sin seriously, she was told, unless the wife isn't doing her job.

Susie Was Told She Needed to Love Bob More

Her lack of love had partly caused his sin, so she needed to go into love overdrive. She needed to immediately pursue him. She needed to lose weight, cook more and better meals, clean the house better, and offer him plenty of passionate, exciting sex. After thirty days of loving him unconditionally, he would repent and stop sinning and love her back.

Susie Was Told to Forgive Bob Quickly and Move On from His Sin

Don't bring up the details. Don't ask questions. Don't vent your emotions. Don't be sad, and, above all, don't be mad. Just stop talking about what he did, how it made you feel, etc. Just be glad he's willing to stay with you.

Susie Was Told It Was a Marriage Problem

The sin was only a symptom of a sick marriage. So don't focus on the sin, but focus on improving the marriage. Work on communication, meeting needs, and doing the love languages.

The Most Popular Christian Approach Is Wrong

Does this advice sound familiar? I'll bet it does. This is far and away the most popular Christian approach to a sinning spouse. It's the advice given whether it is the husband or wife who has committed the sin.

It is the advice most pastors give. It is the advice most Christian therapists give. It is the advice most best-selling Christian authors give.

Twenty years ago, it was the advice I gave to clients. Twenty years ago, I would have told Bob and Susie the same four things. Because that's how I had been taught by my graduate school professors and therapy mentors.

For the first two or three years of my practice, this was the approach I used. It is one of my deepest regrets as I look back on my therapy career. Why? Because this advice, this popular Christian approach to a sinning spouse, is wrong. Wrong. Wrong. Wrong. Wrong.

It is certainly well-meaning, but it *doesn't work*. It damages individuals. It damages marriages that can't afford to be damaged more than they already are. Most of all, it is unbiblical.

If Bob and Susie follow the traditional Christian counseling solution to a sinning spouse, there will be three consequences. I know, because I saw these consequences happen to couples during the first few years of my practice. And I keep seeing them happen to couples who come to me after trying the traditional approach.

First: Susie, the Victim of Bob's Sin, Is Further Victimized

She's forced to take blame for this terrible action she did not do. She's forced to feel guilt for driving her husband to his sinful behavior. She does not recover from the trauma perpetrated on her. She is unable to vent her pain, so it remains inside and gets worse. She is unable to forgive her husband. She is unable to trust her husband. She will always wonder if she's being a good enough wife to keep Bob from sinning again in his area of weakness. She'll be anxious, depressed, insecure, and bitter.

Many pastors, church leaders, and Christian therapists will not confront Bob. They will confront Susie! Susie, who is already reeling from Bob's sin, now gets smashed again by her counselors and helpers. She's told, "Susie, Bob's sin is your fault, and you'd better get to work so he won't go back to his sin." "Susie, not only is Bob's sin your fault, but now it's your fault that you're angry and bitter and won't just let this go."

Bob, the only one who has sinned, gets a free pass! Disgraceful.

Second: Bob Does Not Recover from His Sin

He does not fully confess it. He does not take full responsibility for it. He does not repent of his sin. He does not regain respect for his wife. The deeper personal issues in his life that led to his sin are not uncovered and fixed. He does not make the real changes he needs to make. He stays emotionally attached to his pattern of sinful behavior. He is, in fact, more likely to continue his sin.

THIRD: BOB AND SUSIE'S MARRIAGE DOES NOT RECOVER FROM HIS SIN

Respect and trust are not reestablished. Full forgiveness doesn't happen. Communication remains poor. Their conflict-resolution skills don't improve. They do not develop an intimate connection. The unresolved trauma of the sin continues to separate them.

If Bob and Susie follow the traditional Christian counseling approach to a sinning spouse, their marriage may survive, and I hope it does. But survive is all it will do. It won't thrive. It won't be a great marriage. It will remain a wounded marriage.

If Bob stops his sin, they will probably enjoy a brief honeymoon phase. It'll last from three to six months. "Flight into health" is what we psychologists call it. They think they're over his sin and what it did to Susie and their marriage and their children. Their counselor and pastor think they're over his sin. They're not.

They're running away from the trauma, because neither one really wants to face it and deal with it. After the honeymoon phase, at some point they'll crash and burn. All the consequences I've described will happen. Their attempt to run from Bob's sin, an attempt often encouraged by a pastor or counselor, will fail. His sin will haunt them for the rest of their marriage.

The Belief Behind the Approach

Why is this incorrect, unbiblical approach to a sinning spouse still the most popular one in the Christian community?

There are two reasons.

Reason Number One: Counselors Have Been Trained to Achieve Balance in Marital Therapy

Good marriage work usually demands that you help each partner see his or her role in the relationship problems. It does typically take two to mess things up. "Here's what you're

doing wrong, Bob." "Here's what you're doing wrong, Susie."
In the basic marital case, you ask both spouses to change. In
the basic marital case, you don't zero in on one partner and
demand that he or she change first.

We professionals are taught that this delicate balancing
act applies to all marital cases. It does not! It makes sense for
the basic, garden-variety marital case. It does *not* make sense
when you have a smoking gun: one partner in serious sin.

Reason Number Two: Hardly Anyone Confronts Sin Anymore

There has been a shift in Christian culture in the past fifteen
to twenty years. We've gone from an emphasis on sin and its
destructive power to grace and only grace. Everything is grace,
grace, grace, and forgiveness, forgiveness, forgiveness. But we
have forgotten that for the believer, grace never eliminates the
need for true, complete confession and repentance (see 1 John
1:9). And there is no true repentance without confrontation
of the sinner. And confession of, and repentance for, the sin
creates the possibility of restoration—of fellowship with the
Lord, of a marriage . . .

As Christians, we used to call sin, sin, right to the face of
the sinner. Why did we call sin what it is and confront the
sinner? In order to bring about healthy shame and legitimate
feelings of guilt and brokenness. "The sacrifices of God are a
broken spirit; a broken and a contrite heart, O God, You will
not despise" (Ps. 51:17 NASB). From this comes repentance
(the act of changing one's inner attitude toward something
or someone; from the Greek *metanoeo*, literally, "to change
the mind"). That was biblical love in action; it was "speaking
the truth in love" (Eph. 4:15).

Now, too many of us have redefined sin. Sin is not really
sin. Sin is dysfunction or addiction or bad judgment. These
things can certainly be involved in sin, but sin is rebellion
against God first and foremost. We offer grace and forgive-

ness immediately with no biblical requirements that would bring confession, repentance, restoration, and purity. We want the sinner to feel good, not bad. The subtle message is: your behavior isn't that bad, and you don't have to feel that bad about it.

This is unbiblical wimpiness in action; worst of all, it is heresy.

I know very few pastors, Christian therapists, and Christians who confront sinners head-on. What are their excuses for wimping out?

"I'M AFRAID OF CONFRONTATION"

Confrontation is incredibly intense, difficult, and painful. (It also loses clients, church members, and friends.) But it is what a good counselor does. And it's what a good Christian does. If you are not willing to confront sinners, with loving firmness, you're disobeying the Bible. It doesn't make any difference if the sinner is someone you've been counseling, someone to whom you are married, or someone who is a friend. Your job is to confront the sinner.

"I'M SCARED OF THE SINNER'S WRATH"

It's very common to be blasted and even hated for having the gall to confront a sinner. I've had a lot of ugly scenes in my office: yelling, hostility, rage, venting and raving, and slamming doors. Repentance is very seldom the initial reaction. You've heard the phrase "Shoot the messenger if you don't like the message." The Bible doesn't say don't confront if you think the sinner will have a negative reaction. The Bible says confront the sinner.

"I'M A SINNER, TOO"

You ask yourself, "How can I, with my own sin and problems, confront another person?" Following that reasoning, how can you do anything as a Christian? If you are going to wait until you're perfect before you confront sin, you'll never do it. I'm still waiting for my first sinless day. I'd settle for my first sinless hour.

"I Don't Want to Drive the Sinner Away"

You think if you confront the sinner, you'll lose any influence on him because he'll reject you and leave the process. Or leave the church. Or leave the relationship. The truth is, when you fail to confront the sinner, at that very moment you lose all influence on him. You are weak. You lose respect and power. You have fed his (or her) denial. You are an enabler of the sinner.

If the sinner does bolt, he bolts. But you've done your job. You've told the truth. You've given the sinner the opportunity to confess and repent. Plus, if you're the spouse of the sinner, you've protected and strengthened yourself.

I'm not throwing stones. I used to avoid confronting sinners. I believed these same excuses. Twenty years ago, I realized that the traditional, popular, nonconfrontational, Christian approach to a sinning spouse wasn't working. I turned to the Bible for answers.

What Does the Bible Say?

One of the great confrontations in the Bible is found in 2 Samuel 12:1–13. King David had committed adultery with Bathsheba and then, to cover his sin, had her husband killed. These verses record what happened when God sent the prophet Nathan to confront David and his sin.

Did Nathan excuse David's sin in any way? No. Did Nathan bring up the stress of being a king? No. Did Nathan mention a midlife crisis? No. Did Nathan indicate that Bathsheba seduced David? No. Did Nathan say that David's wives and concubines hadn't met his needs? No. Nathan said, right to David's face, "You are the man!" Using a story of a rich man who stole and slaughtered a poor man's one and only lamb, Nathan nailed David to the wall. It was direct, brutal confrontation.

When actually forced *to face his sin*, *then* David said, "I have sinned against the LORD" (2 Sam. 12:13), and "My sin is always before me. Against you, you only, have I sinned and done what is evil in your sight" (Ps. 51:3–4).

David gives the correct response to Nathan: "I have sinned against the Lord." That's the beginning of healing for every sinner: "I have sinned against the Lord."

In 1 Corinthians 5, the apostle Paul tells the Corinthian church what to do with a male church member who was having sex with his mother (or stepmother). Paul ordered the church to "hand this man over to Satan" (v. 5), kick him out of the church immediately, and shun him. It was direct, brutal confrontation. Why? To produce repentance and restoration.

When someone we know, a fellow Christian, is in serious sin, we don't have to guess at what to do. Jesus Christ, in Matthew 18:15–17, tells us exactly what to do:

> If your brother sins, go and show him his fault in private; if he listens to you, you have won your brother. But if he does not listen to you, take one or two more with you, so that by the mouth of two or three witnesses every fact may be confirmed. If he refuses to listen to them, tell it to the church; and if he refuses to listen even to the church, let him be to you as a Gentile and a tax collector.
>
> NASB

Here's the bottom line: When someone is in serious sin, you confront that person immediately. No excuses and rationalizations are accepted. No one else is to blame but the sinner. The focus is on the sinner and the sin and repentance.

If you are a pastor or counselor, you confront the sinner immediately.

If you are a friend of the sinner, you confront the sinner immediately.

If you are the sinner's spouse, you confront the sinner immediately.

When One Spouse Is in Serious Sin, It's Matthew 18 Time

My approach to adultery and other serious marital sins is based on Matthew 18:15–17. When one spouse is in serious sin, that sin is the smoking gun. It can be adultery. It can be sexual addiction, alcoholism, drug addiction, or workaholism. It can be laziness, irresponsible spending, anger with verbal abuse, physical abuse, or controlling behavior.

Whatever the sin, I zero in on the sinner and make his sin the focus during the first phase of treatment. He'll repent first. He'll confess exactly what he's done and work to fix his problem. He'll help his partner heal from what he's done to her. He'll become the husband God wants him to be.

Later, the other spouse's issues will be addressed. Also, later, the marital issues will be addressed.

Biblically, my approach is based on God's truth. Because it is biblical, it is also practical and effective. It works. The sinning spouse will be first in this process. Then the marriage. You don't have to do a delicate balancing act.

What if you could get one spouse to agree to change first? As that spouse changes, the marriage changes. As that spouse and the marriage change, the other spouse also changes. That's what happens with the Matthew 18 marital approach. Whether it works or not, however, it is biblical. But it works a great deal of the time.

Homework: Chapter 17

1. What serious sin has one of you committed? Adultery, pornography, alcoholism, drug use, gambling, verbal abuse, physical abuse, workaholism, reckless financial irresponsibility . . . ?

2. What impact has this serious sin had on each of you, on your marriage, on your family?

3. What have you done to heal from the trauma of this sin? What steps have you taken and how effective have these steps been?

4. Have you been counseled by someone to follow one or more of these incorrect approaches?
   - The sin is the other person's fault.
   - The other spouse needs to love the sinning spouse more.
   - The other spouse must forgive quickly, cease talking about it, and move on.
   - It is a marriage problem.

5. If you have received any of this counseling advice, how has it worked?

18

Get Angry and Stay Angry

There are thirty minutes left in my individual session with Susie. We've been discussing her husband, Bob, and his serious sin. She has described what she knows so far about his sin, and I've covered the specific steps in my sin recovery program. As I finish the last point of my program, I notice a certain familiar look on her face. I know what she's going to say. It will be a dialogue I've had with hundreds of spouses in my office. Here's how it goes:

Wife: Oh! Oh my! You want my husband and me to do all those things? I mean, all of them?

Me: Yes.

Wife: Well, I . . . I don't think I can be strong enough to follow through.

Me: What do you mean, not "strong enough"? [Actually, I know what she means.]

Wife: I'd have to be really angry to carry out your program.

Me: You're exactly right. To do what I am asking, you'll have to be good and angry. In fact, you'll have to be angrier than you have ever been in your life.

Wife: But I'm not that angry.

Me: You're not that angry? I'd hate to see what he'd have to do to get you angry. His sin has devastated you and devastated your marriage. He thinks saying "I'm sorry" is enough, wants you just to get over it, and isn't sure he wants to come to therapy. Doesn't all that make you angry?

Wife: I was angry at first, but . . . not anymore. Now I'm more sad and hurt.

Me: Sad and hurt feelings are not going to help you, him, or the children. Sad and hurt will keep you stuck in a loveless, trustless marriage. Grieving is important, but you can grieve later. Anger is what you desperately need, and you need it now.

Wife: But, Dr. Clarke, you don't understand. I still love him, and I don't want to lose him. How can I get angry at a man I've loved and given my life to for so many years?

Me: Here's what I understand. Because of his terrible sin, you've already lost him and a genuine marriage. To restore your emotional health, to motivate him to repent and stop the sinful behavior, and to start rebuilding your marriage, you must get angry and stay angry. Getting angry is one of the most loving actions you can do for him. You ought to feel the kind of anger that Jesus felt when he saw his house (the temple) made into a den of robbers when it should have been a house of prayer. Your husband has desecrated your marriage, a sacred institution established by God. If ever there was a time for righteous anger, this is it! Either it is anger over this sin, or the sin—so grievous to the Lord and to you—will go unheeded.

I know some of my advice will sound unchristian to you. Trust me, that's only because you've been misinformed about how Christians are supposed to behave when dealing with sin.

Why You Have Trouble Getting Angry at a Sinning Spouse

So many victims of a sinning spouse are just like Susie. They get angry, but it peters out very quickly. After a brief burst of fury, they turn all weepy and wimpy. They're too nice. Too forgiving. Too sweet. Too passive. Too depressed and devastated. If they keep running down this "anything but anger" path, it's going to be too late to save their marriages.

There's only one way you can motivate your husband to work with you to create a new, healthy marriage out of the ashes of the one he destroyed. You must produce sustained, intense anger. That's easy for me to say, but very difficult for you to do. Like Susie, you need to know three things about anger: (1) why anger is so important in the sin recovery process, (2) why you're having trouble getting and staying angry, and (3) how to get angry and stay angry at your sinning spouse.

"I'm in Denial"

When you first discover his sin, you immediately move into the stage of shock and denial. You simply cannot believe it's true. Not your husband! He wouldn't do this to you! You might waste several weeks stumbling around in a confused, dazed fog. It's easy to get stuck in this stage, because you're trying to protect yourself. You don't want to believe what's happened. Deep down, you may feel that you're not ready to face the truth and the terrible pain that comes with it.

In an instinctive—and quite normal—attempt to minimize the damage and not take his behavior personally, you'll make ridiculous excuses for your husband's sin: "Well, Fred had a bad childhood," or "Fred's going through a midlife crisis."

My response is: "Who cares? There's no excuse for what he's done." You need to take his sin personally because it *is* a personal attack on you.

"I Feel Guilty"

One of the sinning husband's most diabolically clever rationalizations is to blame his sin on his wife, the victim of his sin. He'll say, with a straight face and a tone dripping with just the right amount of fake sadness and sincerity: "If you had been a better wife, if you had met my needs, I wouldn't have done this." Instead of laughing in his face, his wife takes this monstrous, incomprehensible attempt at self-vindication to heart and accepts it. By playing the guilt queen, you play right into his sinful hands. If he can get you to take any part of the blame for his sin, he's sitting pretty. He believes he's in the clear. He's gotten your seal of justification. He doesn't have to be sorry. He doesn't have to stop the sin. He doesn't have to change. Instead, the fault lies with you—you are the one who has caused this and it is you who must change.

Accepting guilt for his sin is simply not true to the facts. You have exactly zero responsibility for his sin. It's 100 percent his fault! He has to answer to God for any behavior he chooses.

The only thing you may be guilty of is enabling him. If you've been aware of his sin and taken no aggressive action, you've been an enabler, and that is your fault. But you can tell him your enabling has come to an end. Now you're going to be a healthy woman and express sustained anger at him and his sin.

Why Anger Is So Important

Even after my brilliant explanation of the obstacles to anger, Susie wasn't completely convinced that she had to get angry with her husband.

"Are you sure?"

I replied, "Yes, I'm sure. I know anger is an absolute necessity in your circumstances."

Here are the reasons I gave her:

First, anger is a normal, healthy, God-given reaction to a traumatic event. The initial shock and denial process suppresses your anger. The anger is there, and you need to get to it because it's how you begin to respond assertively to a serious threat.

Second, getting angry with your sinning spouse is good for you. Without the full and proper expression of anger, you'll never forgive him, not because you don't want to, but because you won't be able to. God designed anger to come first in response to unrighteous behavior. It is the first link in the psychological chain leading to forgiveness. And if you're unable to forgive him, your entire emotional system will become clogged with bitterness, resentment, and hostility.

In the fourth chapter of Ephesians, Paul taught the importance of expressing anger and the consequences if it is not expressed in a safe manner. Read verse 26: "Be angry, and yet do not sin; do not let the sun go down on your anger" (NASB). The anger Paul described is obviously not sinful anger. It is not rage or hostility, but the anger that *precedes* rage and hostility. If you express this anger, it is released, and you won't sin. And, most important, it will keep you from giving Satan "an opportunity" (v. 27 NASB).

It is an entirely different kind of anger from the anger described in Ephesians 4:31: "Get rid of all bitterness, rage and anger, brawling and slander, along with every form of malice." The terms in this verse refer to anger that is sinful and destructive: smoldering, held-in resentment and explosive, violent wrath. I believe the apostle was saying that if you don't express your Ephesians 4:26 anger, you'll end up with Ephesians 4:31 anger. And Ephesians 4:31 anger breaks God's laws and destroys you. It will also prevent you from experiencing Ephesians 4:32 (which immediately follows Paul's teaching about anger): "Be kind to one another, tender-hearted, forgiving each other, just as God in Christ also has forgiven you" (NASB).

The *third* reason to get angry is that it gives you the ability to obey the Bible's instructions on how to confront your husband and his sin. The Matthew 18 road is going to be a very hard road. To follow my sin recovery program, you will have to be strong and tough. And to be strong and tough, you will need to be angry.

Fourth, your anger helps motivate your husband to do the steps in my recovery program. The best thing for him is to rock back and forth in the blast of your righteous anger over his sin. He needs to see that you are furious. You have had it. He is facing an angry, incredibly offended and hurt woman whom he has lost because of his sinful behavior. The only option he is being offered is to work to win you back. This must be made so clear to him that he cannot miss it.

Your sustained anger will cause your husband pain if he has any feelings for you and any spiritual sensitivity. And that pain can result in real change. The causal relationship between pain and change is a biblical concept. Paul, on purpose, hurt the Corinthian Christians with a tough letter (2 Cor. 7:8). But they needed to be hurt! Read about their response to Paul's hurtful letter: "Yet now I am happy, not because you were made sorry, but because your sorrow led you to repentance. For you became sorrowful as God intended and so were not harmed in any way by us. Godly sorrow brings repentance that leads to salvation and leaves no regret, but worldly sorrow brings death" (2 Cor. 7:9–10).

How do you create godly sorrow and repentance in your husband? By being angry! Your anger keeps the *crisis of his sin* at the forefront, the only issue that matters at the moment. You don't want to lessen or defuse the crisis by being only hurt and weak. Change—deep change—occurs only in a crisis. God wants you to stay angry with this intense but rational and coherent anger, and to keep the crisis at a fever pitch until your husband breaks and feels the awesome weight of godly sorrow.

Finally, your anger will help you rebuild your life if your husband does not repent (change his mind, turn from his sin). Anger is your friend in this terrible time. Your God-given friend. If you're forced to shun and separate from him, you must be strong and resilient "enough" to get through it with your sanity, your self-respect, and your self-esteem intact, and with your children intact.

I paused and looked at Susie. She wasn't crying anymore, and there was a new look—a look of determination, and maybe *hope*—on her face. She said, "Okay, I think you're right. I think God wants me to get past the obstacles and get angry at Bob. Can you tell me how to do it?"

I smiled, because I live for such moments in therapy. I responded, "Yes, I can. Helping the victims of sin get angry and stay angry and accomplish what must be done is one of my specialties."

Focus on the Negative

Don't say "I love you" to him. He may say it to you, but don't say it back to him. In fact, don't say anything nice to him at all. Who cares if he runs an errand for you, does a household chore, puts gas in your car, or shows he is "really trying"? Does this make up for his sin and the awful damage it has caused? No.

What you want is a broken and contrite heart. What you want are a million heartfelt apologies, full acceptance of the incredible damage he has done to you and his children, and his every effort at every moment to help your open wounds heal. What you want is a man who will continue following my sin recovery program in the face of your ongoing anger and disgust.

Don't get your hopes up if he suddenly decides he wants to change. Stay pulled back and very leery even if he starts saying and doing the right things. It's too soon to know what he's up to or whether he's sincere. Chances are very good he's just schmoozing you, stalling for time, or easing what's left of his conscience. Do not rush back into his arms. Do not express your hurt and sadness to him. If you're that vulnerable and it turns out he really doesn't want you back, you'll be devastated again. The one last hope you are entertaining will be dashed. Maintain your position as the furious, uncompromising ice queen until he's well on his way to genuine, Holy Spirit–initiated and Holy Spirit–controlled change.

Get the Details of the Sin

One of the reasons you need to know everything about his sin (as I will recommend in Chapter 19) is that it is a powerful, effective way to tap your anger. There is pain in the details, and that pain will fuel your anger. I am not talking here about pitying yourself or hanging on to pain for no reason. The more you know about him and his sin, the angrier you'll be. If he has the unbelievable nerve to refuse to tell you the details of his sin, this attempt to protect himself from (legitimate) feelings of guilt or embarrassment ought to make you even angrier.

Use the Top Ten

Rocky Glisson, my best friend and counseling associate, came up with a great idea we both use in helping victims of sin get in touch with their anger. It's called the Top Ten. We ask the client to write down on an index card the Top Ten bad, painful things that, in his sin, her husband has done to her. She keeps this card with her at all times—in her pocket or purse. When the weepy feelings and the hurt feelings come back and she needs a fresh burst of anger, she just whips out the Top Ten, and it reminds her of the rotten things he has done to her.

Here's one client's Top Ten:

1. He said he never loved me and shouldn't have married me.
2. He blamed me for his miserable, sinful adultery.
3. He betrayed me in the worst possible way.
4. He broke my kids' hearts.
5. He lied to me about his adultery for five solid months.
6. He put me at risk for AIDS and other sexually transmitted diseases.
7. He criticized my weight and appearance.
8. He spent our money on his prostitute.
9. He changed my whole life with his sinful choices.
10. His adultery has forced me to look for a job.

Doesn't reading this list make you mad for her? Make a Top Ten list that goes to the heart of what your husband has done to you, and it will galvanize your internal anger.

Recruit Anger Coaches

You won't be able to get angry and stay angry all by yourself. You will need support and encouragement, and you will need to be accountable to another. Recruit a small core of friends and family to help you to keep angry. Avoid the namby-pamby, weak-kneed, spineless souls who want you to lie down in front of your husband's Mack truck. Let them ruin someone else's life and marriage.

Sign up on your team individuals who are furious with your husband and his behavior. Ask these people to monitor you closely for signs of weakness, passivity, and depression. Ask them to ride you and make sure you're not cutting your husband any slack he hasn't earned with sincere, hard work. Ask them to listen to you vent, and ask them to rally to your side. Ask them to confront your husband when necessary. Ask them to tell you the truth, even when it stings. These are Proverbs 27:5–6 friends:

> Better is open rebuke
> Than love that is concealed.
> Faithful are the wounds of a friend.
>
> NASB

Fake It 'Til You Make It

Even when you're following my anger-inducing steps, it still might take a while for you to get angry. Before you actually feel your anger, you'll need to fake it. Pretend. Act as if you're furious with your husband. As a good friend of mine used to say, "Fake it 'til you make it."

Your husband needs to believe you're angry even if you're not. The fact is, you are angry in there somewhere! Acting angry may even trigger the real anger buried inside. If you can't do anything else, at least pull way back from him. Go into shunning mode. Ignore him. Say nothing to him. He'll interpret this behavior as anger, and that will be good enough until the real McCoy kicks in.

Now that you understand the importance of anger, you're ready to launch into the heart of my recovery-from-sin program. You will require your spouse to perform a series of specific actions if he wants to have a chance to stay in the same home with you. He'll do them all without questioning. Without grumbling. Without any guarantee he'll be able to win you back.

There will be no compromises. No deals. He'll do what you demand, your way, and in your time frame. Period. Or he'll face serious consequences to be spelled out.

In the following chapter I'll take you through my program step-by-step. I want you to know exactly what to do.

Homework: Chapter 18

1. Have you had trouble getting angry and staying angry with your sinning spouse? Why do you think this is? Has this negatively affected your influence in his life?
2. Have you accepted any blame for your spouse's sin? Can you see now that you are zero percent responsible for that sinful behavior?
3. Do your Top Ten on an index card: list the top ten bad, painful things your spouse's sin has done to you.
4. Recruit one or two anger coaches who will help keep you angry until your spouse shows clear evidence of a changed heart and life.

19

How to Heal from a Spouse's Serious Sin

To teach you the steps of recovery from a spouse's serious sin, I'll continue to use Bob and Susie. (If your name is Bob or Susie, I'm sorry. I had to come up with two names, didn't I?) Bob's sin was sexual addiction. Most—in fact, just about all—serious marital sins are addictions. Because addictive sin patterns are so difficult to defeat, a very aggressive approach, for the sinner and the couple, is required.

The marital sin you're facing may be in an area other than sexual, but the steps of recovery are still the same.

I'll begin by giving my response to the four pieces of popular Christian advice Bob and Susie received.

Popular Advice: Susie was told Bob's sin was her fault.

My response: I told Bob his sin was 100 percent his fault.

I made it clear that Bob's sexual addiction had nothing to do with Susie. It was his choice. I said, "Even if Susie was the worst wife in the world, she did nothing to cause you to sin. Susie is responsible for 50 percent of the marriage problems, but any behavior you do is 100 percent your responsibility. If you went out and robbed a bank today, would you blame that on Susie?"

> Popular advice: Susie was told she needed to love Bob more.
>
> My response: I told Bob he was going to have to love Susie more.

I told Susie to stop her pathetic, humiliating efforts to please Bob. I told her to stop chasing Bob. Stop being nice to Bob. Stop killing herself to make him love her again. Why reward the man who ripped her heart out?

By chasing Bob and trying so hard to be a good little wife, she was enabling him. She was agreeing that his sin was her fault. Since he sinned, shouldn't he be the one working harder? The first thing Susie must do is get Bob's respect back. Without respect, there is no love. There is no repentance. Bob won't change. And the marriage is over.

> Popular Advice: Susie was told to forgive Bob quickly and move on from his sinful behavior.
>
> My response: Forgiveness is a process that involves a number of difficult steps.

One godly older woman pulled Susie aside and said, "Don't bring up his sin again, honey." Unfortunately, there are many pastors and Christian therapists who also offer this disastrous advice.

Is this advice recommended for any other trauma work? "As a child you were sexually abused by a neighbor. . . . Just forgive him and quickly move on" (which would even allow you to think it was your fault). Or "A drunk driver killed your daughter. . . . Just forgive him quickly and move on." Or "A financial advisor stole your life savings. . . . Just quickly forgive and move on." Of course not!

To heal from a trauma, you must turn and face it directly. Go over and over the details. Feel and express your emotions. Relive the pain. Process it over and over and over. Go through the stages of grief.

Here are the traumatic-sin recovery steps I guided Bob and Susie through over a two-month period.

Step One: The Sinner Aggressively Attacks the Sin

The first thing we established was Bob's support team. He already had one accountability partner, but I required him to have *two* male accountability partners. Addicts are fighting patterns that are amazingly strong, so their accountability must be beefed up. He ended up choosing a close friend from church and a guy from his twelve-step sexual addiction group. He told them everything he'd done in his life in the sexual addiction area.

If at all possible, one of the accountability partners should be successfully recovering from the same addiction as you. With a fellow addict on the job, you won't be able to fake it. You won't get away with anything, because your partner knows all the addict tricks. He'll ask the right questions. He'll notice things a non-addict will miss. He'll understand what you're going through. He'll nail you. That's what you need.

I told Bob to meet in person at least once a week with each of his accountability partners. Addiction is too strong and sneaky to be held accountable over the phone. In-person meetings are essential for at least one year.

For an addict, a twelve-step group isn't optional. It's absolutely critical. Addicts rarely recover without going to an

243

addiction group for a minimum of one year. The power of a Christ-centered twelve-step group cannot be overstated. I told Bob to find one and quickly, which he did.

I also told Bob to meet with his pastor and tell him everything about his sexual addiction and ask his pastor to create a spiritual growth program for him that would last one year. Even though his faith was weak at the time, he had to start rebuilding it. It could be a small men's Bible study or a one-on-one discipleship relationship with the pastor or a godly older man in the church. This pastor put him in an early morning men's Bible study. I had him tell these men the story of his addiction. Three more Christian men praying for him and holding him accountable couldn't hurt.

I also signed up Susie as a support-team member. It was important that they heal together. I made two things clear about her role. First, she had to heal from the terrible wounds of his sexual sin before she could become a fully supportive and encouraging partner. When she was sufficiently healed, and he had proved he was well on his way to recovery, then she could truly join him in my 90-day program. Until that time—I estimated it would take two to three months—he would have to find empathy and warmth and positive words from his other support-team members.

Second, Susie would never hear the struggles going on in his mind. These thoughts would overwhelm her with pain and continue to rip open the wounds in her heart. However, if he acted out in any sexual way, he'd have to tell her what he did. His day-to-day fantasies and temptations would be shared with his two accountability partners, his twelve-step group, and his men's Bible study group.

Although not always necessary, it is very common for sinning spouses to need individual therapy. It depends on the depth and severity of the addictive sin pattern. I saw Bob in individual therapy during the two months I guided Susie and him through their recovery steps.

Step Two: The Sinner Tells the Spouse the Whole Truth

The sinner has stopped his sinful behavior. He is showing that he respects his wife and that he wants to win her heart back. He seems genuinely broken and has assembled the support team outlined in Step One. So far so good. Now we'll find out whether he's actually serious about his commitment to God and to his wife, because now he has to tell the truth about his sin.

It will be the whole truth and nothing but the truth.

He must reveal the entire, sordid, disgusting story of his sin. All of it. He'll verbally tell his spouse every possible detail he can remember. He will hold nothing back.

Many—in fact, the majority of—pastors and Christian counselors and authors believe strongly that focusing on the details of a serious sin is a mistake. They sincerely believe getting the whole truth out about the sin and discussing it again and again is just too painful and will damage the marriage even further, to the point where it is beyond repair. They want you, the victim of the sin, to pray about his "mistake," forgive, talk about the mistakes each of you has made in the marriage "that led to his sin," and move past that nasty old sinful behavior just as soon as you can. "Don't dredge up this horrible mess; it's past," they will tell you. It's as if by ignoring it, you could forget it.

These well-meaning helpers couldn't be more wrong. Their approach is unsound, not only psychologically and relationally but biblically as well. The Bible teaches open, honest, verbal confession of sin (Matt. 3:6; Mark 1:5; Acts 19:18). The Bible teaches us to confess our sins directly to each other (Matt. 5:23–24; James 5:16). When the Bible describes sinful behavior, the writers often go into detail. The story of David's sin with Bathsheba (2 Samuel 11–12) and his confession of that sin (Psalm 51) is told in detail. Why? Because the details are important.

The details are an essential part of the recovery process. The two of you and your marriage won't heal without them.

How can a fallen husband be truly broken and truly change without a full and open and honest confession of his sin? If any of his sin stays inside, secret and unconfessed, it will slowly destroy him and the marriage. He'll be separated from God and from his spouse by that unconfessed sin. He will not be broken. He will not repent—that is, make a change. What he will do is leave the door of his life open to Satan. And Satan will come in and do terrible, ongoing damage. He must also confess directly to his spouse, because she is the one he harmed most.

How can he gain a clear understanding of his sin and why he did it without directly facing every detail of his sin? What were his motivations that led him to look outside of the marriage? What needs did he want to have met? What family of origin issues, past unresolved painful events, current stressors, personality weaknesses, and poor choices combined to move him to sin? Specifically, how did he allow Satan room to operate? He must find the answers to these questions, or he won't break the power of this sin in his life. He'll be very likely to go back to his sinful behavior. The answers are in the details.

The details are important to the spouse's recovery, too. How can you trust your guilty spouse without knowing exactly what he has done in his sin? You must have the answers to the questions listed in the previous paragraph, or you will never be able to trust him completely ever again. You'll always wonder if he'll do it again. And that's a terrible way to live. Without trust, there is no respect. Without trust and respect there is no genuine vulnerability, love, and intimacy.

How can you completely forgive him if you don't know completely what he's done? You can't forgive what you don't know. You can knowledgeably forgive him only for the specific, confessed sins he committed. Issuing some blanket, general forgiveness for his sin without knowing exactly what those sins are is no more than a feeble attempt to deny reality and—however understandable—avoid pain. This kind of forgiveness is weak, passive, and unbiblical. It will prevent you and him from reaching true healing and reconciliation. Also, he can hide a great deal of what he has done when he uses only generalities. This prevents full disclosure and full responsibility for what he has done. This prevents full healing for both of you.

How can you heal emotionally without confronting and reacting to all his sinful behaviors? You can't! Your pain will remain inside you and eat away at you. The pain will be as great or greater if you must imagine what he did, for what is imagined may be worse than what really happened. You heal psychologically from painful events by reliving those events piece by piece, frame by frame, and expressing your emotions and thoughts about them. This is a fundamental, God-created law of trauma recovery. Most people, including the well-meaning helpers I have mentioned, don't know this law. It is a recognized principle in the professions of psychology and psychiatry. It is the same process I use in therapy to help clients heal from every kind of trauma.

The sinner verbally expressing to his spouse the nature of his sin is important. He'll begin verbally sharing details right after the sin is discovered (and ended) and continue with verbal descriptions of his sinful behavior all the way through the recovery process. He'll answer *all* your questions about his sin with patience, gentleness, kindness, and humility. Or he'll face your righteous wrath. (*Never* will he say anything like, "Are you bringing this up again?" When it stops is entirely up to the victimized spouse in her healing process.)

Step Three: The Document of Sins

But just sharing verbally isn't enough. A crucial piece of my recovery program is the requirement that the sinner write out, *in a letter to the spouse*, the entire story of the sin. I call this the Document of Sins.

I instruct the sinning spouse to put down on paper the most painstakingly researched, detailed, and descriptive account of his sin that he can produce. (The one area in which the specific details are not necessary is the physical part of an adulterous relationship. It is important to know what they did physically in a general way, but not the gory details.)

The sinner can't remember every single detail of his sinful behavior. No one has a memory that good. But with God's help and his own tremendous effort, he can get 85 to 90 percent of the important, major information right. That's good enough. Your intense questioning will take care of the remaining 10 to 15 percent.

I usually give the sinning spouse one week to complete the Document. He writes the letter in private. His spouse does not look on as he works on it. Then he brings it in and *reads* it to his spouse in a session with me. If you choose not to use a therapist, have your spouse read the Document to you in your home. Make sure no one is in the home as he reads it. After the reading, he hands it to his wife. She'll keep it—rereading it and asking questions based on it—for as long as she needs to. This might be a matter of weeks or months.

It's hard to find words to describe therapy sessions in which the Document is read. *Powerful. Agonizing. Painful. Humiliating. Unbelievably intense. Gut-wrenching. Brutal.* All these words apply, but so does the one word that is the point of the process: *healing.* (And let it never, ever be forgotten: this experience is nothing compared to the powerful, agonizing, painful, humiliating, unbelievably intense, brutal, and heartbreaking experience the sin caused the spouse.)

I asked Bob to write a Document of sexual sin. A letter to his wife in which he described all his sinful behavior in as much detail as possible during their marriage from their wedding day to that day. He'd read this letter out loud to his wife in our next session.

This Document of Sins begins the restoration of the marriage. As the marriage is healing, the spouse can come alongside the addict, and they can become one flesh in the recovery. Plus, the intimacy they create during the recovery will meet one of the central needs of the addict. By going through the steps of recovery with his spouse, the addict will find what he so desperately needs: intimacy with God and with his marriage partner.

Here is an abbreviated version of Bob's Document of sexual sin:

> *I am so terribly sorry for all my sexual sins. I never realized how much I was hurting you with my disgusting behavior. I know now what I've done to you, and it's killing me inside. I've told you verbally what I've done, and now I'm putting it in writing.*
>
> *Honey, let me say first that these behaviors are all my fault. One hundred percent my fault. You had nothing to do with my actions. I had this sexual addiction problem even before I met you, and I brought it with me into our marriage. I should have told you the truth and gotten help years ago. I chose to lie to myself and to you, and now we're both paying a huge price for my foolishness.*
>
> *During the first two years of our marriage, I didn't use any pornography. I was so happy with you, and my problem went underground. But after our first child was born, I went back to my old ways. The stress of fatherhood, my new career, and missing your time and attention may have been triggers. But there's no excuse. I decided to go back to pornography.*
>
> *Our baby was about three months old when I started staying up late watching nasty, nudity-filled cable television shows. You'd be surprised what you can find on TV late at night. Movies, public access shows, and the Playboy channel were my favorites. Some channels, like the Playboy one, we didn't subscribe to, but they still came in clear enough to see. I'd usually stay up late*

Friday or Saturday night because I could sleep in the next day. I'd watch for two or three hours, masturbate, then come to bed. I'm sorry. I was stupid.

I would occasionally get a pornographic magazine or two at a certain small grocery store. No one knew me there. This happened about once a month. I'd hide these magazines in my briefcase and look at them when you were out of the house or sleeping. After masturbating, I'd throw them in a dumpster on my way to work.

Dumb. So dumb.

For about six years on and off I'd buy pornographic videos from a seedy video store. About once every two months, I'd go in and buy two. They only cost about ten dollars each. Here are the titles of the ones I remember: [he listed them]. I'd watch these in the middle of the night, masturbate, and then come to bed. I would then throw them in the dumpster on my way to work the next day.

After each episode of viewing pornography and masturbating, I'd feel horribly guilty. I'd beg for God's forgiveness and promise to stop. I could last about two weeks before I started again. I know this sounds pathetic. The addiction had me totally under its control. It was my own stupid fault that I didn't admit my helplessness and get help. The truth is, I wanted to continue.

As you know now, five years ago I started viewing pornography on the Internet. This was like opening the floodgates to my sexual sin. It was bad and harmful before the Internet. After, it became much worse. I couldn't believe how easy it was to find pornography on the Internet. The number of sites seemed endless, the variety was incredible, and most of it was free.

Magazines, television, and porno movies fell to the wayside when I got into Internet porn sites. Late at night or when you and the kids were out of the house,

I'd visit these sites. I felt safe because you weren't too computer savvy. Most weeks I'd view Internet porn about every three or four days. More on the weekends because I had more time.

I'd spend hours, sometimes three or four in a row, surfing the porn sites. Friday night, Saturday night, and usually Sunday afternoon—these were my usual times. But then I started viewing Internet porn on weeknights. I couldn't seem to control myself. Here are the sites I can recall visiting: [he listed them]. I know you printed out a list of most of the ones I visited in the last three months.

I have to tell you something you don't know yet. I went to two strip clubs this past year: [he named them]. Both times, I watched the girls dance for about thirty minutes and then left. I guess I wanted the rush of seeing naked women in person.

Anyway, it didn't do much for me. They weren't attractive. I spent the whole time scared to death someone I knew would see me.

Well, that's it. I'm ashamed beyond words for what I've done. I'm sorry, so very sorry, for my sin. I know I have hurt you worse than anyone has ever hurt you. I know you will have to vent your feelings and ask me questions for as long as it takes. I will do whatever it takes to fix this problem and win you back. Please, please, please hang in there with me as I work through recovery.

When Bob read this letter to Susie in session, it was very intense and very painful. It needed to be. Both were in tears before he finished. The process blew up Satan's lie that Bob's behavior wasn't hurting anyone. The healing for both of them had begun.

I instructed Bob to read this letter as soon as possible to his two accountability partners, his twelve-step group, his pastor, and the three men in his Bible study group. I asked Susie to read the letter to her closest female friend. She needed empathy and prayer support from a trusted confidante who knew the hurts she had suffered.

Step Four: The Document of Response

After the reading of the Document of Sins, the offended spouse will write an honest, heartfelt description of what the sin has done to her. I call this the Document of Response, and I ask the offended spouse to begin writing it immediately after she has heard her husband's Document. She'll read it to her husband one week later in our next session. Again, if you're working without a therapist, read it to your husband at home when just the two of you are on the premises.

This letter tells him what he has done to you. It's a dumping ground for all the horrible pain he has inflicted on you with his sin. Even though you verbalize your feelings before and after the Document of Response, the written expression of the pain opens up the floodgates inside you and begins a deep cleaning of your mind, body, and soul. It forces you to face the specific events of his sin and react to them. In the most graphic, personal way possible, your letter reveals to your husband the damage his actions have caused you.

I urged Susie to not hold back, because full and honest release of emotion is a critical part of the forgiveness process. I instructed her to—emotionally speaking—throw up on paper.

Susie wrote over ten pages straight from her heart. Here are key portions of her Document of Response:

> I don't know if I can find the words to describe what you've done to me by your sexual sin. You have hurt me like no one else could. You have broken my heart. And I don't know if it can be healed.

I feel like I don't even know you. In fact, I don't want to know the person who did all these miserable, hurtful, betraying things. Here's what I do know: You have lost me. There's a good chance you won't get me back, that I can't come back. If you want to win me back, you'd better work like no man has ever worked to change and become the godly husband I want and need.

You see, I thought I had a godly husband. Turns out, I didn't. I had a husband who defiled himself, me, our kids, our marriage, and God over and over again.

My initial shock has turned to rage. How could you keep doing those things you knew were wrong? How could you lie and deceive me for all those years? I am beyond furious at you. You have been so selfish it makes me sick. Why didn't you get help? Why didn't you tell someone?

I think of you watching naked women, and I want to scream in your face, "What are you doing? You've got a wife who loves you! You can see me naked and make love to me!" But no, you took what was mine alone and gave it to these anonymous whores.

I am shaking with anger as I write these words. And underneath the anger is a terrible hurt and sadness. You have wounded me just as if you'd taken a knife and gutted me with it. You, who were supposed to protect and honor and cherish me. Instead, you've damaged me and humiliated me.

I've cried and cried and cried. I feel like I have been torn apart and don't know how I can be put back together again. I don't trust you. I don't feel safe with you. I don't know if I love you. I've taken my heart, my broken and bleeding heart, away from you.

Do your work. Follow the steps of recovery to the letter. Let me know how the process is going. Listen to me every time I want to talk about what you've done to us. Hear me vent and feel my pain. Answer all my questions. Grow in the Lord. You can't change without his help.

I don't offer you any guarantees. "We'll see" is the best I can do.

It was pure agony for both of them when Susie read this letter in our session. But it was the truth. And the truth heals. She had to say it, and he had to hear it. You'll notice there was no empathy or offer of understanding in her response letter. It was venting about his sin and the pain he had caused her, a pain that was still fresh and remained. Nothing else. Emotional expression must come first.

She was a step closer to forgiveness and to becoming a partner in his healing process.

Step Five: The Mode

The next step for the sinner and his spouse is what I call the Mode, a series of brutally honest, intense, and deeply personal conversations about his sinful behavior. The spouse could ask to have one of these talks at any time, and the sinner's response—every time—would always have to be, "Yes, let's talk."

I told Susie that her job was to use these talks to vent her emotions as freely and completely as possible. She was also to ask all the questions that came into her head, with the exception of his fantasies and temptations.

Bob's job in the face of these confrontations was to be patient, kind, loving, understanding, and reassuring. He was to say he was sorry a million and one times—and mean it every time. He was to do his best to answer all her questions, even when she repeated them over and over. This process heals Bob, because he confesses his sin, faces it, and finds out why he did it. This process heals Susie, because she knows exactly what happened and can work through it. This process heals the marriage because respect is restored, they learn how to communicate on a deep level, they learn how to resolve conflict, and they create intimacy.

Popular Advice: Susie was told it was a marriage problem.

My response: It's not a marriage problem, but a sin problem.

Bob sinned. Big-time. It's all about Bob in the initial phase of treatment. He'll do all the repenting. He'll do all the work. He'll do all the changing. Of course, there is marriage work to do. That will come later. After Bob is well on his way to recovery, they will return to my 90-day program.

What If the Sinner Refuses to Do the Recovery Steps?

If the sinning spouse refuses any of these steps, I recommend the offended spouse immediately take the other Matthew 18 actions: confront with one or two witnesses, and then confront him with her church leaders.

If the sinning spouse doesn't respond to these further confrontations, I recommend you prepare to shun (1 Cor. 5:9–11) and separate (Matt. 18:15–17).

Go home and give your husband two warnings. You can give both warnings today or one today and one tomorrow. Don't take more than two days to deliver these two warnings. Time is critical. He has slipped back into serious sin, and we have to act quickly to jar him back to repentance and reality. The longer his sin is allowed to go on without a response from you, the deeper it will get. You can communicate these warnings over the phone, in person, or in a note.

Tell him you're angry and very disappointed by his disgraceful, damaging, and sinful treatment of you. His sin was, by itself, a terrible blow to you. Now his rotten attitude and refusal to abide by Dr. Clarke's recovery program is rubbing salt into your wound. Inform him that you will not tolerate his sin any longer. Make it clear that if he doesn't give you a heartfelt apology and get back on the recovery track, he'll face serious consequences. Don't tell him what the consequences will be. Let him wonder.

Send this message, and don't wait for a response. If you use the phone, hang up without saying good-bye. If you do it in person, say your piece and abruptly walk away. If you write him, don't bring up the letter later or ask for a response.

After your two warnings in a two-day period, if he hasn't responded with brokenness and repentance, move immediately into shunning mode. Don't explain to him what you are doing. Just start shunning him.

Take your wedding ring from your finger, and then shun your husband for the next five full days. Shunning means you go as far as you can in an attempt to act as though he doesn't exist. You don't talk to him. You don't do anything for him. No sex. No laundry. No food.

If he does not break and beg to get back to the recovery steps after the five days of shunning, begin making plans to physically separate from him. Ask him to leave the home. If he refuses, you'll have to leave. (Consult an attorney first to be sure you are protected legally.) If you are unable to leave, continue in the shunning mode.

If you want to know more about my Matthew 18 recovery from marital sin program, get my book *What to Do When Your Spouse Says, I Don't Love You Anymore* (Thomas Nelson, 2002).

Find a Christian therapist who follows my approach. Call Focus on the Family (1-800-A-FAMILY) and get a list of therapists in your area. Ask your pastor for a list. Call each therapist and ask how he or she deals with adultery or whatever serious sin your spouse has committed. If it's the wimpy approach, move on to the next one on the list. Make it clear to each therapist you want my approach followed.

Until you find the right therapist, start implementing my steps of confrontation and recovery.

My approach is brutally tough. So is the devastation caused by the sin. My approach is controversial. It confronts the sinner. It empowers the victimized spouse. It is biblical. It works.

If There Is Physical Abuse

If your spouse is physically abusing you—and just one episode is extremely serious—I want you to leave the home as soon as you possibly can. Tell your support system the truth and ask for help. Take the kids and leave. Do not tell him where you are. Call the police and get a restraining order. Require him to repent and go through a comprehensive and proven anger management program. *Then* you can meet with him in the presence of a Christian therapist and go through the five recovery-from-sin steps.

If the Sinner Continues to Sin

If your sinning spouse stubbornly refuses to repent and follow these recovery steps, I want you to do two things.

First, stay separated (or in shunning mode) and move on with your life. Continue to grow spiritually, build relationships with friends, take care of the kids, and do healthy activities you enjoy. Seek God's direction. In time, God will show you what he wants you to do.

Second, read the rest of this book and follow my 90-day program. These steps will be for you, not for your marriage. You won't share your work with your sinning spouse. You'll do the 90-day action steps for your own insight and healing. You'll be able to see your marriage in a clear, objective light. If your spouse decides to repent, you'll be able to guide him (or her) through the 90-day process. If your spouse refuses to repent, you'll still be a healthier person. And you'll be able to help others improve their marriages.

Homework: Chapter 19

1. Sinning Spouse: Commit to building your support team of two same-sex accountability partners, a twelve-step group, your pastor, a spiritual-growth discipleship group or small group Bible study, and your spouse.
2. Sinning Spouse: Write your Document of Sins and read it out loud to your spouse. Then read it out loud to the other members of your support team.
3. Offended Spouse: Write your Document of Response and read it out loud to your spouse.
4. Offended Spouse: Start doing the Mode (a series of honest, intense conversations about the sinner's behavior), and agree to continue it as long as it takes to produce healing.
5. Offended Spouse: If your spouse refuses to do the recovery steps and refuses to repent, take the actions I have recommended: the other Matthew 18:15–17 confrontations, warn, shun, and separate if possible.

Part 5

With God and a Proven Plan, It's Time to Change Your Marriage

20

Killing Your Goliath

I spent a few weeks wondering how to end this book. What could I say in the final chapter? Frankly, I was stumped. Nothing seemed quite right.

And then Matthew Hartsfield, pastor of Van Dyke Church in Tampa, Florida, saved me. He's a wonderful pastor and a great friend. I should have known Matthew would come through for me.

One of my major culinary gripes over the years was soggy French fries at restaurants. I loathe soggy fries. There's nothing worse than undercooked, limp, doughy fries. They are an outrage and an affront to my digestive system.

I want my fries crispy. Golden brown, crunchy, and firm. Now, that's how fries ought to be! But what could I do about it? I was at the mercy of whatever cook prepared my fries.

A few years ago, Matthew and I were having lunch at our favorite barbecue restaurant. It was time to order, and Matthew went first. He said five magic words that changed my life forever: "Make my fries crispy, please."

I was stunned. Shocked out of my head. Matthew had solved my soggy fries problem. It was genius! Sheer genius! Thanks to Matthew Hartsfield, I have never had to endure even one more soggy restaurant fry since that fateful day.

Little David, Big Goliath

As important as the French fries problem was to me, that is not the focus of this chapter. That was just background.

Matthew gave me my *big idea* for my final chapter when I heard his sermon on David and Goliath. As I was listening to Matthew tell this incredible—outrageous, even—Bible story, I knew I had discovered how to drive home the point of this book.

The account of David and Goliath, found in 1 Samuel 17, is one of the best-known events in the history of the world. The massive giant (over nine feet tall) had taunted the army of Israel for forty days. He challenged the Israelites to send one man out to meet him in hand-to-hand combat to the death. If Goliath won, the Philistine army would be victorious and make slaves of all Israel. If the Israelite soldier won, the Israelite army would win and make slaves of all the Philistines.

All the soldiers of Israel were terrified of Goliath. Not one dared to step forward and fight this fearsome warrior. No one except David, a young shepherd boy with only a sling for a weapon. David courageously went to face and fight Goliath on the battlefield. He killed him with one stone from his sling.

As Matthew spoke that day, I was amazed at the parallels between the David and Goliath account and couples who are struggling in their marriages.

Taking Your Eyes Off God

All the Israelites could see was Goliath. And defeat. And humiliation. They'd taken their eyes away from God. They realized they had no chance to defeat Goliath, this fearsome giant. And they were right. But they had forgotten about God and what he can do. They had forgotten his love for them.

You—wife and husband—who are facing the end of your marriage, you are the Israelites. Your Goliath is your marital problems. Your problems are all you can see. They're big and nasty and look insurmountable. You're totally focused on them.

But you have forgotten who God is and what he can do. "Is anything too difficult for the LORD?" (Gen. 18:14 NASB). And you have forgotten how much he loves you.

Actually, it's not just what God can do for your marriage. It's what he *will* do. God loves you (John 3:16), and he loves your marriage (Gen. 2:24; Mal. 2:14–16). Not only will he save your soul, forgive your sins, and give you a whole new life, he will help you save your marriage and build it into something wonderful.

Humanly speaking, David didn't have a ghost of a chance to defeat Goliath. Humanly speaking, you cannot defeat your marital problems. But you don't have to rely on mere human strength. You can ask God and rely on God's strength. You will have to work, but God is the One who carries the day. With God, you simply can't lose. You have to win.

The Stakes Are Extremely High

Not only had the Israelites taken their eyes away from God and believed everything depended on them, but the stakes were incredibly high for David and the Israelites. If David lost, the Philistines, a very cruel tribe, would make slaves of all Israel. It doesn't get much worse than that.

The stakes for you are incredibly high as well. The most important human relationship in your life, your marriage, is at stake. If you lose, you'll experience the terrible pain of divorce and all its far-reaching consequences. It will be the death of a family unit. Your happiness and joy and peace will be impacted. Your precious children will suffer. One parent, whom they love, will forever be a distant figure. Your family and friends will also suffer.

The rest of your life and the rest of the lives of everyone you know and love will be affected by a divorce.

Facing Your Problems and Taking Action

David faced Goliath head-on and took action. Unlike the entire Israelite army, David did not stay on the sidelines. He sucked it up and went into battle. In fact, he actually *ran* to meet Goliath (1 Sam. 17:48).

You and your spouse need to *face your problems* and *take action* against them. Get off the sidelines and into battle. It's time to stop your misery, think of all the joy and satisfaction you both and your children are missing, and start changing your marriage.

You Have What You Need to Win

I've given you what you need to save your marriage. To build it into a great marriage. And to keep it a great marriage and pass on its lessons to your children and others. I've given you the stones with which to defeat your Goliath.

You don't have to stay miserable. You don't have to get a divorce.

My plan is a proven plan. I didn't make up this Twelve-Week program just hoping it might help you. It's not theory. It's a proven, successful strategy. It's the approach I've used for over twenty years with couples in my psychology practice. It has helped change the marriages of hundreds and hundreds of couples. It will help you and your spouse, too.

My plan will work if this is your first, second, third, or fourth marriage. God wants the marriage you are in now to be the best marriage any couple ever enjoyed.

Marriage was—is—God's idea. It is his supreme gift to humans. (Divorce and friction and unhappiness are man's creation.) So of course it is the desire of God's heart for you to have a great marriage. And for you to help other couples with what you've learned. And, most of all, for you to glorify him with your incredible—outrageous, even—story of restoration and redemption.

You and your spouse have all you need to defeat your Goliath. You have God and you have a proven action plan.

So what are you waiting for?

Frequently Asked Questions

Q. We've tried all kinds of marriage books, marriage seminars, and marriage counseling. Nothing has worked.
What makes your marriage recovery program so special?
Why do you think it will work for us when nothing else
has?

A. My Twelve-Week program is not theory. It works. It has
worked for hundreds of couples in my private practice
over the past twenty-plus years. I believe my program
can work for you, if you both follow the steps.

Q. Your program will require a lot of hard work. I'm not
much of a writer and you require a lot of writing. Does
it have to be so difficult?

A. The good news is my recovery program is only twelve
weeks long. The bad news is it is a very demanding and
intense twelve weeks. But there are no shortcuts to real,
genuine change in a marriage. And don't worry about
your writing. Just do your best. You're not going to
publish it. Your spouse is the only other person who will
see it. It will be destroyed after it serves its important

role. This simple, inexpensive writing exercise may be the only opportunity you will ever have to learn about yourself and heal, and bring healing to your marriage. For such a supremely important thing as your marriage, and something as difficult as marriage, and something in as bad shape as your marriage, what kind of program would you expect? What kind of program would you want? A wimpy, impractical, easy, non-demanding, gutless, and ineffective one? I don't think so.

Q. What if I have different beliefs about God than you do? Your program seems to be based on the Bible and Christianity. What if I follow another faith and religion? Can your program still help me and my marriage?

A. It's true I am a Christian. I have a personal relationship with Jesus Christ and strive to base everything in my life on the Bible. Although I would dearly love to have you come to know Jesus, I believe my *I Don't Want a Divorce* program can significantly help people of all faiths. Your God-given abilities can take you a long way.

Q. How can a really bad marriage be changed in just 90 days?

A. If a couple is not willing to sacrifice and work hard for 90 days, one or both parties believe the marriage is not worth the effort. That's revealing. The 90 days could be a test. If a little spark is created, the couple could feel hope. If it is not some kind of plan like this, what will it be? Or do you just give up? All that is required for this plan is a sincere effort. In a way, trying this program simply means that you lacked some important tools to make a good marriage—like conflict resolution, better communication, help in the area of sex. It means you belong to a club that includes most of us married people. Some of us went to school for six or seven years beyond high school to learn our jobs. You may have invested years in gaining your skills and job. Is *90 days* of hard emotional work that much?

Q. What if we really struggle with some of the weeks in your program and it takes more time to complete the homework? Is it okay to take extra time if we need it?

A. It's perfectly okay to take more time. It's quite common to have trouble with at least a few of my homework assignments. Take the time you need to do a good job.

Q. I've read through all twelve weeks, and frankly, I don't think I can do several of your steps. I have a lot of negative feelings for my spouse right now. You want me to talk with my spouse in four thirty-minute talk times? You want me to do positive, romantic actions for my spouse? Are you kidding?

A. No, I'm not kidding. You can do the behaviors I recommend. Not easily, but you can do them. Force yourself. Pray to God for strength and motivation. Good, healthy feelings and change follow good, healthy actions.

Q. Can we skip some of the weeks? We're either doing okay in these areas or we've done the work before.

A. No skipping allowed. All the steps in my twelve-week process are essential. If you have done some of the steps before, do them again.

Q. I have already forgiven people in my past and my spouse for the harm they did to me. Do I still have to write those letters of forgiveness?

A. Yes, you still have to write those letters of forgiveness. I can't tell you how many clients have told me they have forgiven others, only to discover that they still had leftover resentments that were ruining their marriages. Let's make absolutely sure you have completely forgiven everyone. Do the work.

Q. I have always found it extremely difficult to talk about personal things, about my inner feelings. I am really afraid of being vulnerable. How can I get myself to talk in the Couple Talk Times?

A. Many of us fall into this category. First, just take responsibility for *your* life, good and bad. Since the stakes are so high here, risk as you have never risked before. This is an opportunity that may never come again to become a healthier, happier person as well as to save your marriage.

Q. My spouse wants a divorce and has no intention of doing anything to save the marriage. Why should I bother doing your twelve-week program?

A. My program is not just for your marriage, though I do believe it gives you the best chance to save your relationship. My twelve weeks is for you, too. When you have completed my process, with or without your spouse, you will know you have done everything possible to save your marriage. And you will be able to release your spouse and move forward with confidence into your new life.

Q. I'm married to a husband you call a Stick. He wants to stay married but refuses to make any changes. I'm very unhappy in my marriage, but I feel like God wants me to continue to submit to him and love him no matter what. Am I doing the right thing?

A. No, you aren't. You are enabling him to remain in his sin. God makes it clear in the Bible that you are not to submit to a sinner, but rather, you are to confront a sinner (Matthew 18:15–17).

Q. My spouse is involved in serious sin. If I follow your tough-love approach, won't I push him even further away?

A. There's no way you can push him further away. He's gone now. You have nothing to lose. Plus, you will be obeying the Bible when you take a hard stand against his sinful behavior.

Q. How can I motivate my uncaring husband to want to work on our marriage?

A. Only God can change your husband. All you can do is trust God, stay close to him, and live for him. Trust him for the strength and courage for you to do what this program asks of *you*.

Q. I'm a Christian, but I can't believe that even God can save my marriage.

A. You and many others arrive at this conclusion after turmoil, unkind words, the absence of love, abuse. Jesus himself told his disciples, "With God all things are possible" (Matt. 19:26).

Q. If we are cold and indifferent to one another, and not talking, how do we establish Couple Talk Times?

A. You both will have to act maturely and try something with rules that, if followed, will make a huge difference in communication between you. Considering what you have lost, and what you can lose, what more can you lose by trying to follow the rules?

Q. We do not really enjoy one another's company. Yet you ask us to go on a date?

A. At one time, you dated. You loved being together. Could you go back and act and talk as you did then? Action often results in changed feelings. Happy couples date all through their marriages.

Q. My past and its relationships are things I don't want to ever touch. You are asking me to do the impossible.

271

A. As a psychologist who has heard this hundreds of times, I fully understand the dread you feel. If you do not deal with the past, it will always hurt you and your marriage; it will continue to rob you of happiness personally and as a couple. To insist it is impossible will sentence you to its power of destruction in your marriage and in all your life.

Appendix

Beginning a Relationship with God

I put the most important possible message you could receive here for those of you whose hearts are so broken and who are so consumed by your sadness that you might skip it. And you need it right now, for life and happiness, for eternity, and especially as you begin this difficult path.

Here are the straight facts on how to begin a relationship with God through faith in his Son, Jesus Christ. You are a sinner. So am I. So is everyone. You've made mistakes in your life, haven't you? Well, even one mistake, one sin, separates you from God. On your own, there is no way to reach a holy and perfect God. Romans 3:23 drives home this point: "For all have sinned and fall short of the glory of God."

God could have left you in your pain, condemned, never to know him, to die and go to hell forever. But he didn't do that. God loves you so much that he sent his only Son, Jesus, to earth to die in your place, taking the penalty of your sins:

"There is now no condemnation for those who are in Christ Jesus" (Rom. 8:1). Because Jesus paid the price for your sins, you don't have to be eternally separated from God, from heaven, from all believers in Jesus. "For the wages of sin is death, but the gift of God is eternal life in Christ Jesus our Lord" (Rom. 6:23).

The Bible tells us over and over how we can be forgiven, rescued. It is the central message of the whole Bible:

> Christ died for our sins according to the Scriptures, . . . he was buried, . . . he was raised on the third day.
>
> 1 Corinthians 15:3–4

> Christ Jesus came into the world to save sinners.
>
> 1 Timothy 1:15

The how is very simple: We must believe in Jesus.

> Believe in the Lord Jesus, and you will be saved.
>
> Acts 16:31

> But as many as received Him, to them He gave the right to become the children of God, even to those who believe in His name.
>
> John 1:12 NASB

Do you want all your sins—*all* of them—wiped away? Do you want the peace in your life that only God can give? Do you want his power to energize your life—and your marriage? Do you want to go to heaven when you die?

If you answered yes to these questions, then you are ready to come to Christ.

Repeat the following prayer to begin a relationship with God. (It's not the words you use that will save you. It is what you are choosing in your heart.)

God,

I'm a sinner. I have made mistakes, and I have sinned. I know that my sin separates me from you. I can't reach you on my own. Thank you for sending Jesus as the only way for me to get right with you and know you. I believe that Jesus died on the cross for my sins. I believe that Jesus rose from the dead, proving he is God and has the power to forgive my sins. I'm tired of living my life my way. I now give my life to you, God.

Amen

Other Books by Dr. David Clarke

Men Are Clams, Women Are Crowbars: Understand Your Differences and Make Them Work
A study guide for couples and groups is also available.

A Marriage after God's Own Heart: Achieving the Ultimate: Spiritual Intimacy in Your Marriage
Follow-up materials for couples and groups are also available.

What to Do When Your Spouse Says, I Don't Love You Anymore: An Action Plan to Regain Confidence, Power, and Control

Parenting Isn't for Superheroes: Everyday Strategies for Raising Good Kids

The Total Marriage Makeover: A Proven Plan to Revolutionize Your Marriage

The 6 Steps to Emotional Freedom: Breaking Through to the Life God Wants You to Live

Cinderella Meets the Caveman: Stop the Boredom in Your Marriage and Jump-Start the Passion

Kiss Me Like You Mean It: Solomon's Crazy in Love How-To Manual

To schedule a seminar, order Dr. Clarke's books, download sections from his books and audio of his talks, and access his speaking schedule, please contact:

David Clarke Seminars
www.davidclarkeseminars.com

1-888-516-8844

or

Marriage & Family Enrichment Center
6505 North Himes Avenue
Tampa, FL 33614

Dr. David Clarke is a Christian psychologist, speaker, and the author of eight books, including *Kiss Me Like You Mean It*. A graduate of Dallas Theological Seminary and Western Conservative Baptist Seminary, he has been in full-time private practice for over twenty years. He lives in Florida with his wife, Sandy, and their four children.

William G. Clarke has been a marriage and family therapist for over thirty years. A former Campus Crusade for Christ director and founder of the Marriage and Family Enrichment Center, he lives in Florida with his wife, Kathleen.

Goodbye, Passion?
Not So Fast.

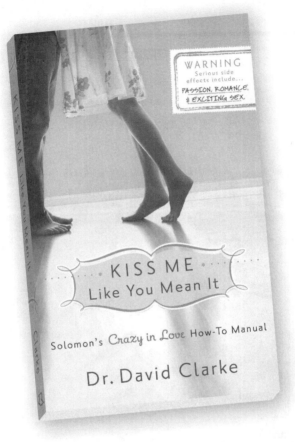

"If you've lost that loving feeling . . . then *Kiss Me Like You Mean It* is a book you'll have a hard time putting down."

—**Gary J. Oliver, PhD**, executive director of The Center for Relationship Enrichment at John Brown University; author of *Mad About Us*

Available wherever books are sold.

A Bestseller That Continues to Change Lives and Relationships

OVER 200,000 COPIES SOLD

Living Successfully with Screwed-Up People

Elizabeth B. Brown

Revell
a division of Baker Publishing Group
www.RevellBooks.com

Available wherever books are sold.

From Bestselling Author and Marriage Counselor
WILLARD F. HARLEY, JR.

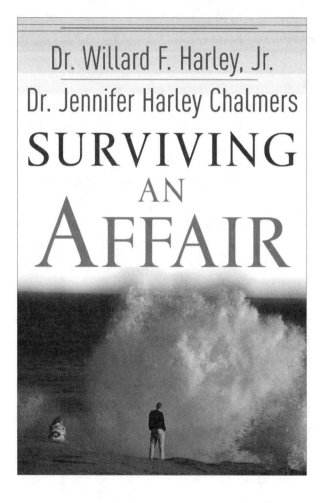

Dr. Willard F. Harley, Jr.
Dr. Jennifer Harley Chalmers

SURVIVING AN AFFAIR

A marriage can survive the crisis of infidelity. Dr. Harley's
step-by-step guidance can minimize suffering and will offer hope.

Revell
a division of Baker Publishing Group
www.RevellBooks.com

Available wherever books are sold.

Be the First
to Hear about
Other New Books
from Revell!

Sign up for announcements about
new and upcoming titles at

www.revellbooks.com/signup

Follow us on twitter
RevellBooks

Join us on facebook.
Revell

Don't miss out on our great reads!

Revell
a division of Baker Publishing Group
www.RevellBooks.com